TOUCHED BY GOD

For Elsie Wigmore,
painter and dear friend

Anthea Dove

Touched by God

the columba press

First published in 2012 by
the columba press
55A Spruce Avenue, Stillorgan Industrial Park,
Blackrock, Co. Dublin

Cover by Bill Bolger
Origination by The Columba Press
Printed by MPG Books Limited

ISBN 978 1 85607 796 5

Introduction

I think of this collection, or rag-bag, some might say, of thoughts and stories and poems, as a sharing of experience. I am old now, and I find myself still a seeker, full of questions, full of wonder. For most of my life I have lived as a practising orthodox Christian, but in recent years I have sensed the touch of God, sometimes gentle, sometimes galvanising, on all sorts of different people and in all sorts of different situations.

In one way or another, we are all touched by God. How can it not be so, since he loves us, since he is love itself? Sadly, some of us may never feel his touch: children born unloved and growing up without love. Sadly too, many of us shuffle or stride though life scarcely aware of that touch. Yet s/he is touching us all the time, through the beauty of nature, the wisdom or kindness of other people, through the happenings in our lives, both tragic and wonderful, through the times when we open ourselves to God in prayer, or reflect on the life of Jesus Christ.

This is a book of random reflections on the touch of God. Sometimes I feel his touch when I am awed by the loveliness of creation, by the sight of the first spring flower or the feel of a small child's body next to mine. But I strongly believe that it is not so much in those things which appeal to our senses, as in situations where there is relationship and where there is action, that God's presence is felt. So it happens that when we hear, in the story that Jesus told, how the father clasped his guilty son in his arms and kissed him, we ourselves experience the touch of God. And I, seeing the unshed tears in Mildred's eyes, her tired face and weary body, after seemingly endless days and nights watching over Jim, her dying son, can feel that touch on her, on Jim, and even on me.

1 Sight

It was the bleakest, deadliest time of year in a dank, dark winter and the wettest January since records began. Day after day the skies, when we could see them, were dull and grey.

One morning I stepped out of my house and saw, in a terracotta pot near my feet, a single hellebore in bloom. I stopped. I was astonished and delighted. The cream-coloured flower stood with her back to me, her face cast down as is the way with these humblest of flowers. I bent down and gently lifted her face. It was exquisite. I thought, how can plants like these have such an unlovely name? I asked my husband, who is the gardener, 'Isn't there another name for them?' 'Well, yes,' he said, 'this is a Lenten Rose.'

The January day was no longer dead and bleak, and I thought, 'How I take my sight for granted!'

2 Blessed by the poor

Father Anthony Storey was not only a very good man; he was a great man. Someone of great intellect, great charm and great heart. When he died, the people whose lives he had touched crowded into the big church for his funeral Mass and when there was no room left, more and more gathered on the street outside. Afterwards, someone made a collection of true stories about him, so many anecdotes revealing his courage, his wisdom, his humour, his generosity, his compassion, his brilliance and his lifelong fight against injustice.

A few months after this booklet had been published, I heard another true story about Tony. But this time I saw him from a different angle. I learnt something not about how good Tony was to other people, but how good, at the beginning of his ministry, others had been to him.

It happened when he was a young curate, working in a poor parish in the north-east of England. My friend, Rosie, told me how, when she was a child, this tall, handsome, beautifully-spoken young priest used to visit her family regularly. They were the only Catholic family in a street of sixteen houses where everyone was poor, where it was a struggle for every family to feed their children and keep them warm. Father Storey quickly made friends with everyone who lived on that street. 'They all loved him,' Rosie told me, 'but they started to worry about him.'

Tony lived in the presbytery with a tyrannical old priest who treated him harshly. Possibly he thought he was 'making a man' of him; we shall never know. But the women on Rosie's street soon noticed how thin Father Storey was and how eagerly he tucked into any food that was put before him. Frequently he was invited to share the family's meals, and the neighbours were quick to contribute, discreetly, with extra bread and vegetables. Then the women realised that the priest always wore the same black suit: it was shiny in places and threadbare in others. So they saved from what little they had and clubbed together to buy him a new suit.

Except for Rosie's mother, these women were not churchgoers, but they knew a good man when they saw one, and who is to say that it wasn't some of their goodness and generosity that went towards making him the great man he eventually became? I believe that God touched Tony through these simple open-hearted women.

3 Zachary

When my son had to be away for several weeks, he asked me to go and stay with his wife, to help her with the children. Sarah was a newborn baby then, and Zachary over a year old.

I woke in the night. I heard the baby cry, and his mother hurry to pick her up for her feed. Only minutes later, I heard the sound of Zachary's voice. He wanted his mother too. I flung on my dressing gown and hurried into Zak's room. He was half asleep, only half-crying. I lifted him down from the cot, surprised at the solid weight of him, and quickly carried him downstairs and into the sitting room. I thought that if I could soothe him his mother would be able to go back to sleep after feeding the baby.

I sat on the sofa and let Zachary flop down onto my chest. He had scarcely opened his eyes and simply relaxed, his little body a deadweight on mine. I remember how uncomfortable I was, and how seriously happy. Part of me wondered how long I could hold him in this position; part of me wanted him to stay for ever! I had already had five babies of my own, one of them Zak's father. I had loved them and held them and delighted in their warmth and sweetness. But this was something different. Could it have been the contrast between the warmth of the child's body and the chill of the unheated room, not to mention the stiffness of my own body? But no; it was two things: the simple pleasure of touch – Zachary's body welded to mine – and his complete self-abandonment and trust in me.

4 Peacemaking

Last year I went for a visit, too short a visit, to Corrymeela, the centre for reconciliation in Northern Ireland. Staying there was a wonderful, life-giving experience in so many ways: the warmth of the welcome, the kindness of the staff, the inspiring beauty of the Croí, the chapel which is at the heart (*croí* means heart) of the prayer and the work which goes on day after day. But over and above all these things was the spirit of reconciliation. Corrymeela was founded when the troubles in Northern Ireland were at their worst, and the idea was to provide a place and an atmosphere where Catholics and Protestants could meet together in safety and get to know one another as people. We were told stories, stories that moved me to tears over and over again. We learnt of the courage and the suffering of the men and women who came to Corrymeela, of their generosity of heart and, most moving of all, of their capacity to let go of hatred and suspicion and freely forgive. I cannot remember now the names and details of these stories, but one that stands out in my memory was about a couple I will call Maggie and Frank. Maggie was a Catholic whose only daughter had been killed by a Protestant. Frank was a Protestant whose young son had been murdered by a gang of Catholic youths. Maggie and Frank were invited to Corrymeela. Reluctant and burning with hatred, nonetheless they were persuaded to come and together with others who had suffered similar tragedies, they listened to one another's stories.

At the end of the weekend each person was invited to light a candle, not in memory of their own child or loved one, but in memory of someone dear to their erstwhile enemy. Maggie tearfully lit her candle for Frank's son Davy, and then it was Frank's turn. He said, 'I'm lighting my candle for Maggie's daughter, Bridget.' His voice was shaking, and as he bent down with the taper, his hand too began to shake. He tried, and tried again to light the candle, but he couldn't steady himself. When his third attempt failed, Maggie came over to him, placed her hand on top of his and gently guided him towards the candle. It caught light and blazed among all the others. The touch of God was felt at Corrymeela that day.

5 Power

I am lying in my bed with my electric blanket switched on when I hear the first shriek of a fierce north wind gusting around my chimney. I smile contentedly and snuggle further beneath my duvet, relishing the warmth and the comfort. I love listening to the wind, any wind, but especially one as thunderous and powerful as this one. I want to stay awake, and listen. I remember Psalm 104 and its triumphant praise of God: 'You walk on the wings of the wind', and I think of God's tremendous power for good.

I lie still, listening, until my thoughts abruptly turn in another direction entirely, and I begin to wonder, is there anyone out there in the streets of my town, in a doorway perhaps or huddled under the bridge? Is there somebody homeless out there in the bitter cold? What is it like for them? How do they feel about this howling wind?

6 Out of the mouths

I was once asked to teach a group of young children, aged four to five, about God. There were several foreign children in the class: a number of nose-to-the-grindstone, hard-working little Poles, and a few lazy, fun-loving Italians. I told them that God made our wonderful world and all the plants and animals in it.

Then, one day when school was over, Antonietta came back into the classroom with her mother. She was a beautiful child, already considerably overweight, with black glossy curls, bright brown eyes, rosy cheeks and a wonderful beaming smile. She was clearly bursting with excitement and she was carefully carrying something covered in wrapping paper. Triumphantly, she handed me a glorious pot plant.

I tried to express my surprise and pleasure, but now Antonietta had – unusually for her – a serious expression on her face. Looking at me directly, she announced, 'God made it!'

I thought, if I never succeed in teaching anything to anyone again, at least I've got through to one person, this once. And I didn't say, what perhaps I should have said: 'Praise the Lord!'

7 Rohan

There were a lot of people at the party,
perhaps a hundred. Some I knew:
most were strangers. But I noticed him,
because he was so beautiful,
not just the shape and colour of his face,
but in the way he moved with careless grace,
like a much younger boy.
He was laughing with his friends and moved away.

Afterwards, when I thought about the party,
I remembered him. And now I know his name:
Rohan.

Soon after the party, Rohan died in an accident. In so much sorrow, so much love, surely God was there.

8 The beautiful funeral

The young priest said
it was not an occasion for sadness,
it was a celebration of your life.
And when it was all over
I heard people say
it was a beautiful funeral.
They said your parents were wonderfully brave,
and Matty and Ruth so touching,
reading their poems and prayers
without a tremor.
But I did not find
your funeral beautiful.
I found it terrible.
I could not celebrate your life, Jessie.
How could I?
Oh, I know that sentimentality
is out of place,
and amid all this nobility and dignity
self-pity is disgraceful, deplorable,
but I can't help longing, so fiercely, darling,
that someone would think about me,
understand what it's like
to be your Gran
and to have to go on living
without you.

9 Flo

Flo is a good friend of mine. In winter she made a sort of 'double-glazing' for the windows of our cottage, made of sailcloth suspended from a pole: her idea, which worked surprisingly well. She is a feisty young woman who loves life, and is enthusiastic about singing and baking and gardening and long walks in the country, about children and old people. In other words Flo is a great person to have around. We have never spoken about God or religion or the power of prayer. It would not occur to Flo to go to church or chapel on a Sunday. But when a mutual friend of ours had some news that saddened him, he showed me a card she had sent to him. Inside she had written:

'Sometimes, I think of someone special: I think of golden sunshine light and I try to hold them in that sunshine light.'

What can that be but prayer?

10 Two photographs

We made a decision to try to adopt a child who had no-one to love him or her, and we were telephoned by the agency to say that there was a three-year-old boy, 'black as the ace of spades' available for adoption. We went to the Children's Home and were introduced to Peter. He was not 'black as the ace of spades' but the colour of milk chocolate with curly hair and a solemn expression. Chris took a photograph of him that day. He looks unanimated, bewildered. His eyes are dull and there are 'bags' under them.

We were told we should foster Peter for a year before we could adopt him, so we took him home to meet our children, then aged fourteen, twelve, eleven and ten. I have another photo taken when he had been part of our family for perhaps two months. Peter is sitting facing the camera, clasped close in the arms of his big brother Sam. Both look happy; Peter looks bright-eyed and eager.

It is very hard to say whether our decision to adopt Peter was the right one for him, because he has had a very rough ride as an adult, struggling with drugs, racism and depression, but I still treasure the two photographs because they seem to symbolise the huge impact that a sense of belonging, of security, of being loved, can have on a child, or indeed anyone, who is starved of these things.

11 Grass

By mid-July, there is no longer the profusion of wild flowers in the dales and on the moors that there was in April, May and June. There are still dog roses in the hedges and foxgloves by the wayside, but even so, the overall impression is one of greenness.

Perhaps this is why it is at this time of the year that I begin to notice the grass more, to see with a more discerning eye the fields of wheat and barley and the different grasses that grow and blow on the moors. I tend to think of grass as ordinary, but when I see its delicate beauty backlit by the sun and quivering in the wind, I am transfixed, as in the way I am by the sight of a mist of bluebells or a sea of buttercups.

The other day I watched a televised match at Wimbledon. I don't play tennis, and I am not usually an enthusiastic supporter, but this was different. For the first time in many years a female British tennis player was doing well. She was not a professional; only a 'junior', but she was British and she was only fourteen, fighting to win the Junior Championship, her opponent a sixteen-year-old from Thailand. I noticed that Laura had an attractive face as well as being very talented, and I became increasingly keen for her to win. But there was a moment when I forgot about tennis, my national pride and the pretty girl. It was when the sun backlit her hair and a slight breeze set it dancing, just like the grass of the field.

Again, I was transfixed, and I thought, it is not only that God's creation is beautiful and intricate, but he has made a wonderful connectedness among all things, such as a girl's hair and the grass of the field.

12 The Work of God

I didn't know her name
or whether she was beautiful.
From where I stood I could only see her hair
framing her face
and catching the light from behind
and quivering
like music or water.
And I thought of the grass that grows on the moor,
for sometimes it, too, trembles
and catches the sunlight and dances in the wind.

And I know these things
to be the work of God.

13 Reggie

It's clear that Jesus holds children in affection and they also have great significance for him. I met Reggie only once, but he has great significance for me.

Reggie is a child of the world. I have no idea what he would write on a form which asked for his race: he is certainly part-Mexican, part Puerto-Rican, part Afro-American, and I guess there are a few other bloodlines in his make-up. The only sure fact is that he is not white.

At twelve years old, Reggie has a beautiful, expressive face. His hair is a mass of tumbling black curls and his eyes are a deep brown. His body is sturdy, his energy limitless.

When I met Reggie, he was with five adults, including his grandparents. We all went for a walk down to the beach, the grown-ups engaged in serious conversation, Reggie running and skipping ahead and bounding back like an exuberant puppy. On the beach he persuaded his granny to take a bet with him. He wagered £5 that he could stand waist-high in the sea for five minutes, and she accepted his bet. The rest of us stood part of the way down the cliff path as Grandma and Reggie walked across the sand.

It was a cold day, the sea an uninviting waveless grey. I wouldn't have dreamt of dipping as much as a toe in the water for a second. But Reggie took off his shoes and shirt and strode unflinching, into the sea, wearing his striped shorts and red baseball cap. Some yards out, when the water was up to his waist, he turned to face us and stood, waving his arms from time to time.

As the minutes ticked by, we, the spectators, grew more and more anxious for him and began to shout to his grandmother, a good Christian lady, telling her to have mercy on the poor child. But Grandma stood her ground and only when five minutes were up did she relent.

Reggie came out of the sea, smiling. 'It was hard at first,' he said, 'but I thought to myself, "Cold is only a feeling".' He ran ahead, his wet shorts flapping against his thighs, not pausing to hear his grandfather say, 'Ah, but feelings are important.'

14 Missed chance

We were on our way home from holiday and we had a long, tiring journey ahead of us. We came round a corner and saw a young man hoping to hitch a lift. I just had time to register that he was very tall and dressed in unusually bright clothes. He smiled at us and we smiled back. Then we drove on.

I said, 'I wish we had given him a lift.'

Chris said, 'Would you like me to turn back?'

I said, 'No.'

Why did I say no? For several good reasons. The car was very full with our luggage on the back seat. I knew Chris was already quite tired and could do without complications. It was difficult to turn round on that busy road, and in nearly every news bulletin it seemed there was mention of knife stabbings and we knew nothing about this young man.

But were these reasons or excuses? We could have turned round, we could have made room in our car. I knew we had missed the opportunity to meet someone new, to be touched by his life. We had turned our backs on the chance to show kindness.

I still wish we had stopped. Who knows what might have happened? Who knows what might have happened to the Rich Young Man if he hadn't turned away?

15 Weardale

Dipping over the horizon
from Teesdale, wild and beautiful,
we gasped at Weardale,
wilder and still more beautiful,
spread out, below and beyond,
a wide and lovely space:
no buildings, not even fields or trees,
no people,
only the subtle curves and colours of the hills
laid bare in the sunlight,
naked and voluptuous
yet chaste and understated.
When I see the work of God's hands,
I wonder, like the psalmist
'What are we, that you keep us in mind?'

16 A woman of infinite variety

We are all called to change and grow, but in most people such alterations are barely perceptible, even to themselves. When I think of Dorothy, I smile, feeling a glow of affection for her. She is now nearing ninety, and claiming to be almost retired.

I first met Dorothy when we were both *burra memsahibs*, that is the wives of senior company managers in southern India. Like me, Dorothy lived in a beautiful house in a beautiful garden, waited on by several servants, all ready to do our bidding. She and Dennis were considerably older than us, and soon after they retired from India, Dennis died. They were then living in a smart area of London, and Dorothy decided it was time she took a job, so, being highly-qualified, she joined the Civil Service. It was responsible and interesting work, but after a few years she reached the official retiring age.

She left work and went to live in Brixton which was at that time a notorious trouble spot. At once Dorothy became involved in the community, working tirelessly against racism and befriending a great number of black people who quickly realised that in spite of her colour, her accent and her impeccable manners, she was no 'do-gooder' but a genuine, committed fighter for their rights.

All this was immediately clear when I went to visit her. Several neighbours came and went, needing advice or sympathy; her sitting room was alarmingly filled with piles of papers: letters, articles and leaflets. But somehow there was time for us to 'catch up' and to enjoy the simple but delicious meal she had prepared.

Afterwards we went into the garden and this was a revelation. At the front the house faced straight onto the street, and it was joined to the other houses on either side so there was no hint of a garden but at the back there was this green, enclosed space, quite small, with a patch of lawn in the middle and a great number of flowers. Some I knew: roses, lilies, lily of the valley, sanguinaria, but what struck me most was that every flower was white. It was a white garden, grown and blooming in the middle of a black community. It was a place of profound tranquillity created by one of the busiest people I know.

17 Holy place

Several times in my life I have been a pilgrim, walking with others towards a very special destination, to a shrine or sacred building which commemorates someone to be revered, a saint or a person who inspired others.

Inevitably, in such a pilgrimage there is an element of organisation, of timing, of the suitability of the terrain and the weather. Even more inevitably, there is something concrete to mark the end of our journey: a grave, a statue, a chapel, or even a book, something which represents the person we have come to venerate, or perhaps simply remember more intensely for a little while.

A few days ago I went for a walk with friends through woodland which took us along the side of a little river. It was a warm and sunny day, but it had been raining heavily for a few days and the stream was full and flowing fast. The trees were beautiful, their leaves golden in the autumn sunshine. Unusually, for early October, there was no wind.

Far from the road, we saw a sign saying 'Quaker Burial Ground', so we took a detour and walked along a track until we found the place. It was enclosed by an old stone wall, and inside there was 'nothing'. There were no visible graves, just a simple wooden bench, grass underfoot and several trees, lovely as the trees outside in the wood.

There were eleven of us. No one spoke. We walked quietly among the trees and each found a place to sit or stand. I don't know how long we stayed there. The only sound was the river, a short distance away, otherwise the space was perfectly still. I think we all shared the same thought: 'This is a holy place'.

18 Solomon

This year, in the familiar Dales, I came across a place quite hidden away, where wild flowers grow in abundance. I saw flowers that are beautiful and delicate and extremely rare. Like Wordsworth's violet they seem 'born to blush unseen'. The friend I was with was excited and enchanted: we had discovered treasure.

But another day, in the same area, we found another flower which delighted me even more. This one is not like the 'lilies of the field' which Jesus compared to Solomon in all his glory. It would be easy to miss seeing it because it is so tiny, its white petals forming the shape of a star, and it grows only where lead has been mined. Lead mining was gruelling work, and cruel: long hours, miserable conditions, pitiful wages, a heavy toll on strength and health. The mines are grassed over now, the hillsides they once scarred grow green and beautiful. The tiny, starry leadwort goes on blooming, a meek symbol of triumph over adversity.

19 Exile

John and Anselme are both refugees from Cameroon. They know that if they are deported back there they will be imprisoned, tortured and probably killed. The UK Border Agency have twice put Anselme on a plane to return to Cameroon, but each time he resisted so hard that the airlines would not take him and his escorts had to take him back to the detention centre. On both occasions he was badly beaten. Not surprisingly, he is very afraid, but John said this to me:

'I told Anselme that if I am sent back to Cameroon and I am killed, I will have come to England and found that there are some very wonderful people here, and I didn't expect that I would have this chance to know this. And if I am killed, I will know that it is God's will.'

John is not a professor of philosophy; he is a coach driver, but he has an amazing acceptance of what life has brought him, a dignity, wisdom and peacefulness which are rare in any person, let alone someone whose life is so precarious.

20 Sparrow falling

This afternoon as I was walking across the fields to my friend's house, a small bird flew onto a fence post quite close to me. It stayed for only a few seconds, but I think I recognised a fledgling blue tit, fluffy with pretty markings and blue the predominant colour. My spirits lifted at the sight, but sank again only minutes later when I walked through the open door of Jill's cottage to find a dead sparrow on the doormat and the beautiful grey-furred, green-eyed cat crouched near by. Was he triumphant or guilty? Impossible to tell.

Life is like this, I told myself, and I thought of my daughter Pippa. Not so long ago she was a bride, radiantly happy, loving and loved. For her the future stretched ahead, full of promise. Now she is the victim of cancer, and having suffered a double mastect - omy, she is waiting to start chemotherapy. As for me, an old woman, I can only watch, seeing the bluebird of happiness and the lifeless sparrow. I can only watch what happens to Pippa and like any mother wish it was me. And where is God? I believe he is there, a presence in joy, a presence in suffering, watching with compassion.

21 Refugee

I long for my homeland:
for those I love
and those who love me.
I long to live again
with my own people,
my simple, joyous, warm people,
and I long to speak my own language,
and sing my own songs
and sit in the sunshine.

But I am afraid.
I fear the people of power
in this cold, grey country,
this alien land,
will return me to my homeland,
my beloved homeland,
where certain death awaits me.

And so I live here,
trying to pray,
trying to hope,
trying to sing,
and all the time afraid,
and all the time longing,
with all my heart, for home.

22 Children

Mandy said: it is a beautiful lake
with every kind of water-lily.
I thought: this will be a blessing.
For I was seeking solitude,
serenity, tranquillity
and contemplation.
But I found none of these.
There was a beautiful lake, yes,
and every kind of water-lily.
But there were also children, hundreds of them,
in brightly coloured garments, with loud voices,
running in all directions across the grass,
noisy and happy in the sunshine.
And I thought: this is a different kind of blessing:
theirs, and mine too.

23 Pamela

We regulars at St Anne's used to laugh at Pamela. She was so ridiculously pious. After she received Holy Communion she would fall to her knees, and stay there, hands clasped and eyes closed for several minutes. This was all very well until old Mrs Wetherby tripped over Pamela's legs and fell, crying out with a swear word that shocked everybody.

Pamela prayed fervently, not only to God and Jesus, but to Mary and every saint you could think of, and probably more. Her missal was full of holy pictures which scattered in her wake. But she was nice and she was harmless. 'Eleven pence in the shilling' was our verdict and we were fond of her in a way.

Then, one afternoon I met my friend Clare. Hesitatingly, I asked after her daughter. Jodi was a drug addict who made her respectable parents' lives miserable and anxious. Jodi was still in her teens but completely out of control. Her craving for drugs had driven her to crime. She stole from her mother and trashed her bedroom, then when her father, unable to take any more, banned her from living at home, she roamed the streets, breaking into houses and reacting with violence to anyone who got in her way.

Her bewildered, unhappy parents continued to love Jodi. But they knew she was homeless and seriously damaging her health.

When I asked after Jodi I was surprised to realise that Clare looked slightly less strained and anxious than the last time we met.

'Oh I've been so worried,' she said. 'It's so bitterly cold and I feel dreadful not letting her into the house. I kept imagining her freezing to death and I know it's not even her fault. She can't help being an addict. I couldn't sleep for worrying.' Clare paused, and then she actually smiled.

'But then Pamela found her,' she said. 'She's a saint, an absolute saint. She lets Jodi and some of the other girls sleep in her back room and she even feeds them sometimes, though goodness

knows how she manages when she is living on the dole herself.'
I stared at Clare. 'Pamela?' I said. 'You can't mean Pamela White?'
'You know her?' Clare asked eagerly.
'Well, I thought I did,' I said.

24 Joy and grief

It has been an emotional day. It began with the most joyous wedding I have ever attended, full of colour, music, laughter and happy tears. The beautiful young bride wore a gown that was made, by hand, by her friend, the handsome groom wore a brilliant gilet he had found in a charity shop. The guests were many and motley, including octogenarians and infants. I came away feeling reinvigorated and uplifted.

But in the evening our friend John phoned to say he is dying. The four of us: John and Paddy, Chris and I, have been close friends for a long time; of a similar age and with so much in common. We hold one another in great affection. John says he has had a very happy life and he is neither sad nor afraid, but of course we are sad to think of losing him. I went to bed sober and sorrowful.

25 Nothing

I stand beside this big man, this courteous, dignified African, who suffers repeatedly from nightmares, who is the victim of the unfathomable workings of the Home Office and Immigration, who lives in fear for his wife and in terror for his own life, and I think: I know nothing, and I can do nothing.

26 Darkness

For a long time
I have equated darkness with evil,
because I know God is light.
But yesterday I drove deep into the country,
and while it was still light,
I went to my friend's house.
Much later I came away
and only a few metres
from her lighted windows
I found myself in darkness so complete
I couldn't see my car
or the road beneath my feet.
I knew then that darkness was beautiful
and friendly and strangely comforting.
And I know that God, who is light,
is there in the darkness too.

27 The Ring of Light

A priest friend from Chicago wrote and told me
he would be spending his Christmas with the prostitutes.
A friend in Chile told me
she got her food from the queue in a shanty town.
A friend in South Africa sent an email,
describing her celebration with abused children.
A friend in England told me he had lived in Jerusalem,
with Arabs, Jews, Catholics and Protestants together.
And he said,
'There is a ring of light encircling the world,
light from the spirit of those
whose hearts are made of flesh,
who hunger and thirst for righteousness
and live, not for wealth or power or security,
but for the peace and goodness of humanity,
the peace and goodness of our world,
our earth.'

28 Mystery

We often walk out into the country, and I find the beauty of the moors and woods and becks and skies uplifting and inspiring. But the other day I walked high above Egton Bridge, on a road I have often taken, and there was a different experience.

It was a crisp, cold day; there was plenty of ice underfoot and decorating the hedges and walls. The blue sky was cloudless and there was a brilliant sun.

I looked across the landscape and found that I couldn't see everything clearly; in some places a white mist was shrouding houses and trees. Rather than this being a disappointment, somehow it was an enhancement. The view was even more beautiful than when I have seen it before: the mist lent it a serenity and peacefulness.

And I realised that for me at least, faith is like this. In an inexplicable way mystery actually enhances beauty and there is no need to struggle to understand everything: the Trinity, the Last Coming, even the problem of evil. All these are best left unfathomable.

Just as the mist magically made our surroundings that morning more beautiful, so the mystery of our God reveals him to be at once more believable and more wonderful.

29 Unremarkable

Out in the countryside
I was watching a small brown body
sitting there so still,
an unremarkable bird.
And I thought of Mrs Jones at home,
another little body.
She wears a brown hat and a brown overcoat
and scuttles along to the shops with downcast eyes.

Someone whispered, pointing to my bird,
'Look, a skylark!'
She heard the sound, opened her wings
and soared higher and higher up into the sky,
all the while singing.
It seemed the sort of music
angels might sing in praise of God.

And I wondered,
could there be more to Mrs Jones
than meets the eye?

30 Giving

I was very impressed when my friend, Bronwen, told me this true
story:

Elinor was in her eighties when one night, about two
o'clock in the morning, she was disturbed by a noise in the
kitchen. Calmly putting on her dressing gown, she went
downstairs to find a burglar in her sitting room.

When he saw her, he was startled, but before he could
decide whether to attack her or run away, Elinor smiled
and spoke to him courteously. 'Look around and choose
something for yourself that you would like,' she said. 'I will
gladly give it to you.'

31 Neighbour

When my daughter Pippa had cancer, she found coping with the chemotherapy very tough. One day she confided to her neighbour, Gill, that she felt too tired and too sick to prepare a meal for her husband and children who would be coming home hungry for their evening meal.

Gill was a vegan, and the very thought of a butcher's shop was nauseating to her. However, because she knew that Pippa's family particularly liked eating beef, she steeled herself to go and buy some steak and kidney. Avoiding looking at it, touching it, or above all, smelling it as far as she could, Gill managed to make a big steak pie.

She was rewarded by the delight on the children's faces when she carried it into their kitchen, and was very happy to see Pippa, who had been eating hardly anything for days, enjoying her offering.

32 Bus journey

For several reasons we decided to give up our car and use public transport instead. I wasn't really looking forward to this. Friends had told me of waiting in the cold for a bus that was very late or occasionally didn't turn up at all. Others talked of having to sit next to smelly people, and one complained of finding a piece of chewing gum stuck to his seat.

We often used our car to drive out into the country to a place where we could walk, and we thought this would be something we would badly miss. But we knew there is a bus which travels round most of the villages outside our town two or three times a day, and we decided to try it.

The bus arrived punctually. The driver was friendly and the bus was clean and I began to realise the advantage a bus has over a car: because my seat was so much higher I could enjoy more of the scenery. I had a really good view of the gardens and fields as we passed. But this was not the chief bonus of bus travel that struck me that day.

Like a hospital ward, a bus is a great leveller. There is no hierarchy, no class system among the passengers, but in a small country bus like this, there is a good deal of humour and cheerful gossip.

I know very well that all my experiences of public transport will not be like this one but I did come home happy.

33 Outcast

When we lived in India we used to visit friends who lived in a place that was paradise on earth. Their house could only be reached by boat and it was charming to look at, white-washed with a thatched roof of coconut leaves and a pillared verandah. In front there was a small lake with hundreds of water lilies and there were coconut palms everywhere.

There was only one downside: no running water and so no flush lavatories. Instead we had what the jolly Brits called 'thunderboxes', and they were emptied for us every day by the sweeper.

In all the visits we made I never once saw the sweeper properly. I have a memory of a wisp of a person slipping noiselessly by, clearly hoping not to be seen. It's not just that sweepers are considered to be the lowest of the low, which is bad enough, but what makes it even worse: that's the way so many of them see themselves, as utterly worthless.

When I think of the outcast in that white man's beautiful home, I think of Hagar, who was cast out into the wilderness.

We, in the west, and of course, nowadays, enlightened Hindus too, see the caste system as deplorable and outrageous. But perhaps we are not always aware of our own tendencies to judge and discriminate. I have to ask myself: are there people I would rather not welcome into my house because of the way they look, speak or smell?

34 Surprise

I love surprises, and today I had one.

On holiday, I went with a friend to a small town, a large village, perhaps, on the west coast of Wales. It was a dreary day and rain was pouring down. I didn't expect much of this place, which we were only passing through, and when we parked in a back street, my impression of ordinariness, heightened by the weather, was confirmed. My companion wanted to explore and set off but I didn't join him, preferring to stay warm and dry in the car.

After about ten minutes he came back, happy and a little bit excited. 'Come with me,' he said. I got out of the car and realised that not only had it stopped raining, but the clouds, just like the sea, now revealed different shades of grey, from charcoal to silver.

It was a strangely moving sight, but now we walked round the corner to find a little harbour bright with many-coloured boats. Beyond it was a low green hill, and framing the harbour, with a small church in the middle, were three rows of houses, painted in pastel shades.

It was enchanting.

35 Friend of sinners

Sheila and her husband Tim chose to live on a notorious housing estate in one of those cities which is the butt of jokes because it is considered to be 'the pits', usually by people who have never been there. Statistics might seem to bear out much criticism: levels of unemployment, poor health and crime are alarmingly high.

But of course there are certain things statistics can't measure, such as the warmth and grit of people who have lived in that city for generations, or the courage and optimism of those few like Sheila and Tim who are determined to make a difference.

They rented a house on this sink estate, and although vandals set it on fire within a month of their arrival, they returned to it as soon as repairs were complete. Very gradually, they began to win the trust of their neighbours.

There was a small church on the estate, but it was unused, because no priest was willing to live in the vicarage. After several years of requests and negotiations, Tim and Sheila were allowed to use the empty vicarage as a community centre.

I was puzzled by this story and asked: 'But why can't you get a vicar?'

Sheila smiled sadly. 'Because there is no-one who will go where Jesus went,' she said.

36 Belonging

Standing on Hadrian's Wall,
I seem to experience
a new consciousness
of time, of distance, of connectedness,
and also a new conception
of belonging.
To whom does this bleak beauty,
this crumbling masonry belong?
To the military Romans?
To the ubiquitous Americans
hungry for history?
Or simply to the wild birds
and the wilder winds
that blew so long ago
and blow now?
Along the wall
I saw plants growing:
forget-me-nots and foxgloves
that do not belong here
but shelter and thrive
in the crannies of the wall
ready to bloom in the summer.
And I thought: all of it,
everything, always
belongs only to God.

37 Wild freedom

I am an old woman, living in a small cottage far away from any metropolis or place likely to feature in the national or international news. I no longer drive a car, and haven't travelled any distance from my home for several months.

In view of this I was more than a little surprised when a friend, after thinking about my life and my future, prescribed 'wild freedom' as the way ahead for me. Those two words conjure up for me pictures of jungle exploration or white water rafting, or abandoned dancing to Abba in the film *Mamma Mia*.

Quiet, book-loving, serious, unexciting, unexcitable: these are the sort of adjectives many people might use to describe me, adjectives surely quite appropriate for someone of my age and yet ...

And yet what my friend said delighted me because it confirmed what I had come to see for myself. Now I realise that there is a whole world to explore, a world that is all the easier to explore in solitude and quietness. It is the world of imagination, of memory, of dreams, of possibility, of openness to God however and whenever he chooses to touch me. It is the world where I can discover and change and grow, a world unconstrained by convention or rules or fear, where my spirit can fly with outstretched wings.

This is not about me, it is about and for all who are old and physically restricted. So I am grateful for the perceptiveness of my friend.

38 Midsummer

I went for a walk today and was conscious of my cup overflowing. It was beautiful: blue sky and sunshine, weather warm with a refreshing breeze. Birds were singing all along the way. There were dog roses in the hedges and splashes of buttercups at the roadside. To the south and north were undulating fields lush in their greenness and everywhere trees, their leaves still bright and fresh.

I thought how blessed I am, one of the privileged few who walk the earth. It is true that I have friends far richer than me, far healthier, younger and certainly more beautiful. But like them I too belong to the elite: the comparatively few in the world who have enough to eat, plenty of water, guaranteed warmth and a roof over our heads. I have known this terrible truth for a long time, but it was only today that I realised that I also have the great privilege of being able to enjoy the beauty of creation, like the midsummer beauty of today which is a benison on my spirit.

39 Stephen

Last winter a strange young man came to our small town. He was very noticeable not only for his appearance, but because he literally spent hours standing on the kerb looking into space. He is still there, months later, still standing, with a blue sleeping bag under his arm.

When I first saw him I actually felt a little afraid. He is a big man, very tall with masses of black curly hair which he wears long with a beard. I suppose I thought, as I guess many people thought, that he might be dangerous.

But I also felt sorry for him and worried about him. I wondered if he had any friends, any money, or a roof to sleep under. I noticed that nobody spoke to him, and so at length I plucked up the courage to say 'Good morning!' as I passed by. He didn't respond, so next day when I passed I tried again, and this time he half smiled and said 'Hello'. This went on for a few days until this morning.

I was a bit out of sorts. It was a cold, grey day and I was tired from the after-effects of a migraine. But when I saw the man standing alone as usual and ignored by passers-by, I thought, it's time to make a bit more effort.

I said 'Good morning!' and moved so that he was facing me directly. When he responded I said, 'What is your name?' He smiled and said 'Stephen'. I smiled back. 'I have a son called Stephen!' I said and told him my name. Then he gave me a smile I will never forget, his eyes intent on my face and so full of warmth and concern that I felt blessed and uplifted. It was an extraordinary, grace-filled moment.

As I walked on, I realised that I had been thinking of myself as someone being kind and doing good. Never for a second had it occurred to me that I was to be the beneficiary of Stephen's kindness and goodness.

40 Tap on the shoulder

It felt as though God tapped me on the shoulder. I was walking up the garden path, as I have done many thousands of times, and as almost always, I was walking quickly and purposefully, focused on what had to be done indoors.

It was when I reached the last foxglove, which is roughly as tall as me, that I felt impelled to stop in my tracks.

I understood that if there was anything important to be done, it was not to be the work inside the house, it was not work at all, nor was it a duty. It was simply to savour the happiness of the moment, to pause and look around me at the loveliness everywhere which I take for granted. Not just the foxgloves, the roses and the sweet peas, the pretty alchemilla – Ladies Mantle – that strays on to the path and brushes my bare ankles as I walk by, the bumble bees and the blackbirds, the blue sky, the sunshine and the peacefulness. I breathed the summer air and I became aware of a deep thankfulness.

41 The kingdom of God

Once I felt the touch of God very powerfully. It happened when I lived in a small village. I was responsible for organising a function and for this reason I was standing alone on the stage. Suddenly, as I looked down on all those people, men, women and children, I was filled with an overwhelming feeling of affection, compassion and tenderness; in other words love. I felt for an instant that I had an insight into how God loves us, of how his love is perfect, unconditional an undiscriminating.

Even while I was held in this miraculous moment, I was reflecting upon the complete change of attitude in myself. Now there was no difference in my feelings towards any of the people present: people who had irritated or annoyed me before were as lovable as my dearest friends.

After only a few moments, just seconds perhaps, the brilliance of this experience faded and I was 'myself' again, but what I had learnt has stayed with me and I try still, unsuccessfully, to live by it. That night it seemed to me that I had glimpsed the kingdom of God where we all belong to one Father: where we judge no-one, where we understand that each person is conditioned by his/her history and experience. In the kingdom there is no hierarchy and no competition.

Sometimes people who know me as a Christian are shocked and dismayed if I tell them that I believe God loves Muslims, Buddhists and atheists as much as he loves Christians. But how can it not be so, when even the humblest parents are careful to give love to all their children equally?

42 A child's eye view

When I was reflecting on the piece I have called 'The kingdom of God', I realised that the experience I described there happened over forty years ago. It is still vivid in my memory, and so is something not dissimilar which occurred around seventy years ago.

I was about eight years old, running across a field, in the sunshine by myself, and brimful of happiness. I knew nothing of violence or war, of poverty or riches; I had only the faintest idea of how people other than my own family and friends lived. So perhaps it is excusable that when I climbed to the top of a familiar stone stile and stood still and gazed at the world spread below and around me I felt that all was well with the world.

I looked down and across to the little town where my father worked, and around at the fields spread as far as I could see until they merged with the moors, and I felt an upsurge of feeling – of intense joy, wonder, thankfulness and, yes, rightness.

I didn't know that a war was looming, that people in my town were hungry and out of work, unable to pay for a doctor. I was ignorant of all these things and innocent too. I knew very little, but I think that perhaps, even so, I knew God then.

43 Encounter

When I stood in the room with John, and listened to his story, I was taken unawares by a sudden shift in the focus of my life. Things that had seemed paramount to me for so long, things like love and relationship, suddenly paled and faded in their signific - ance before the harsh reality that was being presented to me.

This quiet, dignified, soft-spoken man was very afraid, because he knew that he was likely to suffer torture and death in only a short while. He was clinging on to hope, and I was catapulted into a new dimension: this was a matter of life and death for John, and by association for me. It was only too real. I seemed to feel not only his fear, but the coming pain too.

Wise people say: 'Do not let yourself become emotionally involved'. Not to do so, in this case, would surely be callous. I felt I had no choice but to embrace John, literally, yes, but also with the concentration of my whole being.

44 *Little brown children*

Countries like Britain are now, at least in our cities, multicultural. There is no longer anything odd or remarkable about sitting next to an African, Indian or Japanese person on a bus. It is true that some people are still nervous of the stranger they perceive to be 'other' or 'not like us', but even those who live in all-white villages or small towns are familiar with brown and black faces on our television screens.

It was not at all like this in the small country parish where I grew up. At the age of five, I was introduced in my Church of England primary school to a song which went something like this:

Over the sea there are little brown children,
Fathers and mothers and children dear,
Who have not heard of the message of Jesus,
Telling the children that God is near.

I was filled with a mixture of amazement and pity, trying to imagine those boys and girls who looked so different and lived so far away.

Then, last week, I went to see the celebrated film *Slumdog Millionaire*. I was enchanted by the scene in which hundreds of little brown children, dressed in brightly-coloured tatters, race barefoot along the muddy paths between the thousand or so makeshift shacks of the vast shanty town outside Mumbai. They were running away from the authorities, sure-footed and fast, frightened yet somehow joyous.

I thought: what wonderful diversity there is in our world, and what terrible injustice, still.

45 Potential

When Mary made her powerful gesture of breaking the jar of costly ointment to anoint Jesus, she surely knew the effect it would have on people around her. But she 'did what it was in her power to do'.

When I read this account in Mark's gospel, my thoughts turned to Barack Obama and his famous slogan, 'Yes, we can!'

How many of us invest in our own potential, or even admit to having any potential? We are very good at hiding our lights under bushels, at pretending we are lacking in any particular talent or skill. Sometimes this is due to modesty, but more often, I would guess, and thinking of myself, to timidity.

But always the Marys and Obamas of this world are an inspiration to us all. Let's not be afraid to catch the vision, to pursue the dream, to be and to give everything we can.

46 The fight for Silas

I have just come out of a fight. I feel exhausted and wrung out, and not elated, because we have not won, we have just managed to gain a lull in the struggle.

We, that is a group of men and women, some of them friends and some unknown to one another, have been battling to save Silas, a young African, from being deported. He was due to be taken, at 1 a.m. this morning, from Heathrow back to his own country where he will almost certainly be killed.

I am not going to tell his story here; suffice it to say that he is courageous and prayerful and desperately dependent on our help. When I say 'help', I have done very little myself. I have stayed in the background, shopping, cooking and washing up, in other words getting on with the practical things that have to be done, so that others can concentrate on the deliberations, discussions, emails, faxes and telephone calls that have been flying in different directions across the country. I have also spent time praying for Silas, praying and observing.

There is a great deal of anger when these things happen, anger that is righteous but also important because it is directed against the people in power who use their authority with indiscriminate cruelty. I have been part of this frustration, exasperation and rage for some time, but during these past days of trying to save Silas, I have come to see something very different.

What has struck me most powerfully is the sheer goodness of some people who have made a real sacrifice in terms of their own well-being, who have worked tirelessly, with unstinting commitment, to help this young man, including those who knew him well as a friend, and those who have never met him. Silas's deportation has been deferred – for a day, a week or a month. We have no way of knowing yet.

But out of the misery and horror of this situation, something nourishing has come to light. The justifiable anger has been superseded by something altogether more fruitful: a shared passion and compassion.

Sometimes, though for me extremely rarely, something 'happens' when we pray and we have a powerful sense of God's presence.

47 The explosion

I saw the sun rise over the sea;
an explosion of colour, beauty and light,
I seemed to see the glory of God.
I stood transfixed, dazzled, dwarfed,
and worshipped my Creator.

A smaller, greater miracle;
just me sitting quietly,
listening for God, waiting on him.
Suddenly – an explosion
without noise or terror,
an explosion in my heart
of light and life and peace,
flooding all my being,
abandoning me to him entirely,
he in me and I in him.

48 Maundy Thursday in the village church

The people came:
all sorts of folk,
people of the parish,
visitors, outsiders
and those with a different slant on faith.
The preacher told us
the kingdom of God was very near
and then he washed our feet.
Afterwards
we ate and drank together
and we talked and laughed
and went out into the starry night
alive and alight
because the stone was already rolled away
and we had glimpsed the kingdom.

49 Communing with bees

Many people talk to their pets, and often believe that their dog or cat at least partially understands what they are saying. Others enjoy talking to plants and my six-year-old grandson told his mother that he had heard trees talking to one another.

I was moved by these and other similar stories, but one that I found particularly startling and yet convincing was the first-hand account of an old man. Jim, and his friend Dick were both bee-keepers, and when Dick, who was older by a good few years, became frail and unable to manage his bees anymore, Jim offered to come over and look after the hives on a regular basis. This meant that Dick could still keep his bees and the arrangement made him happy.

After some time Dick died, and after the funeral Jim went down to Dick's hives. It was in the middle of winter and very cold but Jim sat down on the ground close to the hives and put his hand on top of one of them. He knew the bees were asleep and there was no sound from the hive.

After a while Jim spoke. He said, 'I have come to tell you that Dick has died and we have just buried him.'

At first nothing happened. The drear afternoon remained silent and still. But then, gradually, Jim became aware of the sound of movement and within a few minutes the bees began to pour out of their hives. Jim stayed quite still. The bees began to crawl over his hand and then up his arm and over his face. He closed his mouth and eyes and the bees made a soft blanket to cover his face. Unafraid and strangely at peace, Jim stayed like this until it felt right to speak again. 'Thank you' he said.

In response the bees stirred and then gently went back to their hives, to settle into sleep once more.

50 Fashion

I was listening to *Woman's Hour* on the radio when an item came up about the latest fashion. Two enthusiastic young women were enlightening the presenter, telling her what to wear and what not to wear, informing her that the colour of the season is beige, and that the one indispensable item of fashion is a camel coat which should on no account be worn buttoned, but hanging loosely from the shoulder.

I thought this was daft and wondered how grown women can get so obsessive about such things. I thought about the whole mass of the world's population who come into the category of The Poor: the unemployed in developed countries, the starving in developing ones, sanctuary seekers striving to exist on thirty-five pounds a week. Can we believe that by any stretch of the imagination any of these people care what colour is fashionable this season?

I know which side of the great divide between rich and poor is my side and I feel helpless and ashamed. I won't be wearing beige this season, because I have a good red coat. But I do have a coat.

51 Order

I love wild places; wild flowers, and wild animals, hares and deer, red squirrels, curlews and skylarks. I like forests where the paths have not been scrupulously tidied, and slightly overgrown cottage gardens where treasures are to be discovered in the undergrowth. What I do not like are the trim flower beds we often see in parks, where flowers are planted to grow in disciplined rows, frequently in harsh reds and yellows.

But when I went for a familiar walk towards the end of July, I had a surprise. It was a route I take often, all through the year, observing the seasonal changes. On this particular day nature seemed slightly disconsolate. The leaves in the hedges had lost their freshness and looked a little dusty and tired. The only flowers I saw were white: bindweed, moon daisies and yarrow.

But when I reached the hamlet at the end of my walk, everything changed. There is a beck with fields on either side in the little village, and there someone had planted a garden, consisting of two plots. I had noticed it each time I passed, and admired the neat rows of careful planting. This day I glanced down as I always did, and stopped, amazed. Both plots had matured: the vegetables looked tempting and ready for harvesting: the flowers were a blaze of rainbow colours. Here were the fruits, not just of careful husbandry, but of loving care. Those small gardens were easily the most beautiful things I saw on my walk that day, except perhaps for the wild sky above us and the wild sea beyond.

52 Cherry tree

Over and over again I call to mind this poem by A E Housman:

Loveliest of trees, the cherry now
is hung with bloom along the bough
and stands about the woodland ride
wearing white for Eastertide.

And since to look at things in bloom
fifty springs are little room,
about the woodland I will go
to see the cherry hung with snow.

Because I am old, I often think, as Housman did, that this may be the last time I see a bluebell wood, or a certain beautiful dale, or even a particular person. There is, of course, a sadness in this way of thinking, but it also brings an intensity of experience and appreciation. As it happens, like Housman, I do have a special love for cherry trees, of their white blossom in Spring and brightly-coloured leaves in Autumn, and when our little son, Benjamin died, we planted a weeping cherry over his grave.

I don't agree with Housman that the cherry is the loveliest of trees. I don't even like the ones with pink blossom that look like candy floss. Apple blossom is surely as beautiful and so many trees are wonderful in their different ways, that it seems invidious to compare them.

But what stays in my mind above and beyond anything else to do with the cherry tree is this ancient piece of wisdom:
'"Speak to us of God", the cherry tree was asked,
and the cherry tree blossomed.'

What does this mean for us? Perhaps that God brings out all that is good and beautiful in us, if only we will let him, a thought which seems to coincide with the wise words taken from Jewish Scripture by Pablo Neruda: 'God says: "I would like to do to you what Spring does to the cherry tree".'

53 Lilla Cross

Regretfully, I cannot claim any Scottish blood, but that is not the reason why the celebration of the New Year is not especially important to me. I have seen in the New Year in various ways: at a village party, at a prayer vigil, in the houses of friends, but most often, in bed, asleep.

Last year I did something different. I went on a journey, a pilgrimage. It took three hours, so it is quite ridiculous to compare it with the journey of the Magi, which must have been incredibly long, challenging and exhausting, and must have taken years to complete.

However, I imagine that their journey and mine do have some elements in common, namely struggle, anxiety and a climax that was a revelation, an epiphany, for the wise men, life-changing, for me as unforgettable as anything can be.

We were walking to Lilla Cross which stands in peaceful isolation in the North York Moors, literally miles from anywhere. It is the oldest Christian cross in the north of England, and was carved and put in place in memory of Lilla. When, in the early seventh century, the enemies of King Edwin made an attempt on his life, Lilla stood in front of Edwin and took the blow which would have killed him. Not long afterwards, Edwin became a Christian and had the cross raised in honour of his faithful servant. It stands on a slight hillock, surrounded by wild moorland.

Seven of us met at the parking place. I knew three of them, but the other three were strangers to me, and because it was a very dark night, I didn't see them at all, before, during or after the walk. But I did get to know them, because they took good care of me as the only woman and one of the oldest in the group.

It was not only dark but cold too. For me it was hard-going, more or less uphill all the way, and the ground was uneven. The track had been gouged out by numerous illegal bikers, leaving deep, muddy puddles along the way. I was afraid I wouldn't be able to keep up.

We reached Lilla Cross at two minutes to midnight. The seven of us circled the cross and together we prayed. Then we shared hot drinks and biscuits, perhaps a kind of eucharist. In spite of the dark and cold and the mud, I was keenly aware of warmth and light, the kindness of strangers and the glory of God.

54 Mulgrave woods

November, ninety years and more
since the great and dreadful war came to an end,
we walked up the track through the woods,
rain falling unremittingly.
And I wondered,
was so much water spilled
in the tears of all the widows,
sweethearts, mothers and friends
of the lost generation?
And I saw
below the taller, darker trees, already bare,
the unbearable beauty of young beeches,
without benefit or benison of sunlight,
yet ablaze and golden,
and thought,
here is gallantry,
once more.

55 Beyond expectation

Just occasionally, we are touched by joyous experiences so powerful that we feel jolted from our everyday way of being, and then after that first delightful shock, we are lulled into a strange sense of numb tranquillity.

Such happenings are rare, and so for me it was astonishing that one Friday my spirit was so shaken twice in one day.

The first experience was one of overwhelming beauty. It was a balmy morning in early May, bright and warm with sunshine, when I was taken to see a place beautiful beyond my imaginings. It was quiet except for continuous birdsong, and everything seemed new and alive and growing: wild flowers, wisteria clinging to the old brick of the Tudor house, magnificent trees proudly displaying their fresh new leaves, fields and meadows beyond. I stood there alone, savouring the fulness, the loveliness, the space and the peace.

And afterwards, on the way to Cambridge, I reflected on the morning, slowly reliving the experience, full of gratitude and wonder.

We were in Cambridge to see our son Peter, whom we hadn't seen for some time. Peter is our adopted son, large and black and dreadlocked, who might be described as a 'lost boy', one of those who fell victim to drugs and a life of crime and prison. He has been damaged by life and badly scarred by what as happened to him. Anger seems to smoulder near the surface of his composure.

In view of all this we approached the meeting with some apprehension, but we were in for a surprise. Peter was nothing short of wonderful: courteous, considerate, articulate, gentle and most striking of all, deeply affectionate. After lunch we walked through the town together. All the while, Peter held my arm, and when we parted, he hugged me fiercely.

Afterwards, I reflected on the afternoon, slowly reliving the experience, full of gratitude and wonder.

I am in awe at the power of nature and of beauty to move us, but still more deeply in awe of the power of kindness to transform us.

56 Sunset over the city

Almost everyone, except the blind, has seen a beautiful sunset and surely marvelled at its glory. The sun sets all over the world, every day, and has done since time began. Poets have described sunrise and sunset, artists have painted them, photographs have captured their beauty. So I ask myself, is there any point in adding my own sunset reflection to this plethora of description? But I write when I am touched or moved by an experience, however familiar it may be to others, and so I want to try to describe what was for me something unique and humbling.

We were travelling by train from Cheltenham to Scarborough, and we had reserved our places. We were very tired after a long and stressful day, and we were grateful to find our seats were at the front of the carriage in a place reserved for passengers in wheel chairs, so there was plenty of leg room. Our pleasure was short-lived, however, because the large labrador opposite us began to suffer from diarrhoea, and the stench was overwhelming. I was more than ready to get off at Leeds, where we were changing trains. As we approached the station I looked across at the high-rise flats and commented on their ugliness. We alighted, to discover that we had missed our connection by one minute and had to wait another hour. There is a high walkway at Leeds station which has glass sides, giving clear views of the platforms one way and the city on the other. I sat on a bench, my back to the city, while Chris stood facing me. He suddenly looked up and said 'Look!' I turned round to see something so beautiful that I felt shaken and stunned.

The whole sky was a canvas of vibrant colours, orange, pink and gold with little wispy, silvery clouds. On either side black jagged buildings framed this picture of loveliness. I stood and stared, acutely aware of my littleness and of the greatness of God who created this. I stared, in an attitude of worship, until inevitably, the colours began to fade and the clouds to fragment. I realised that the irritations of the day had also faded and fragmented to nothing, in the face of the glory I had witnessed.

57 The goodness of people

When Eileen, the single mother of three young children, was diagnosed with cancer, she prayed very hard to be healed. She went through the processes of chemo and radiotherapy, and was full of gratitude to God when her consultant told her she was completely cleared and cured. Seven years later, when her children were in their teens, the cancer returned. Eileen felt totally disillusioned, let down and betrayed. She gave up her faith in God. She endured the treatment again, and recovered again, but five years later the cancer came back. This time the treatment was harder; Eileen was no longer young and strong. Her children were grown up and she didn't have the incentive to fight the cancer. Some way into the treatment, she began to go to the local day hospice, where a eucharistic service was held every Wednesday. One day she told her story to one of the hospice nurses, who listened with sympathy but was surprised too. 'You said you have lost your faith?' she said. 'Yes, I did. For a while I hated anything to do with religion.' Then Eileen smiled. 'But now I'm so happy and grateful, because my faith as come back and it's stronger than before.' 'I don't understand,' said the nurse. 'What happened?' Eileen smiled again. 'Nothing really happened,' she said, 'but I started to come here. And I saw it, time after time, the goodness of people. I knew it could only come from God, even though sometimes it shines through people who have no knowledge of him. I have been so blessed.'

58 Another Mary

I am writing this in Advent, a season when my thoughts sometimes turn to Mary, the Mother of God. One day I was reflecting on the beautiful, anonymous and probably medieval poem which says of Jesus:

He came al so stille
there his mother was
as dew in Aprille
that falleth on the grass
and wondering was it really so peaceable
and comfortable for Mary?

That evening I was watching a television programme called *Dispatches*. It was concerned with the plight of refugee children. One of the children was a Ugandan girl called Mary.

For me there was a terrible irony in this. Mary, the Mother of God, suffered cruelly as she stood at the foot of the cross. As Simeon had predicted, a sword pierced her soul. It is crude and unreal to make comparisons, but certainly I have never seen such savage wounds as the young Ugandan Mary bore on her body. Even the professional doctor who had examined her scars said that in fourteen years of doing such work she had never seen more horrific evidence of torture.

Yet worse than this was the damage done to Mary's spirit. She had endured such degradation that she believed she was no longer human. Many knives had pierced her body; many swords had pierced her soul.

59 Advent

I seem to be longing with all my heart
to kneel at the Crib and worship.
I long to pour out my love for the child
my saviour, brother and friend,
newborn and fragile, needy and dependent.
Then, suddenly, like the glorious song of the angels
shattering the quiet Bethlehem skies,
a new thought comes to me, and I understand,
that much as I long for him.
he longs for me, too,
even me,
and with a greater longing.

60 December roses

These roses are real,
not dead,
nor made of plastic or silk.
They have stayed in the tall glass
absolutely still, for days,
their pale pink petals, sweetly curved like an infant's cheek,
not falling.
Outside, the snowflakes whirl
and little gusts of icy air
blow through the cracks in the doors and the window frames
of the old house.
These are December roses
perhaps the last of the year.
They have the papery beauty of an old face
and I cannot bring myself to throw them away.

61 The meaning of Christmas

Last year I went to my local bookshop where they stock greetings cards and I pointed out that among all the hundreds of beautiful seasonal cards there was not one which referred to the birth of Christ. This year it was different: there was one card which had these words emblazoned across the front: 'Aren't we forgetting the real meaning of Christmas – the birth of Santa!', but in addition there were several attractive depictions of the incarnation.

I began to question myself: what is the real meaning of Christmas for me? For a long time, unthinkingly, I had considered it to be the time when we remember that God became man about two thousand years ago, born to Mary in a stable in Bethlehem. Christmas is like a birthday, I thought. Indeed it is a birthday, when we remember and give thanks for a significant event.

But this week I saw Christmas rather differently. Since early childhood there have been certain carols which I have sung, in various places and circumstances, every year: *Away in a Manger, Come All Ye Faithful, In the bleak Midwinter* and several others which I know by heart. And for some reason, one verse of one of these familiar carols, *O Little Town of Bethlehem*, came unbidden into my head two days ago:

How silently, how silently
the wondrous gift is given.
So God imparts to human hearts
the blessings of his heaven.
No ear may hear his coming
but in this world of sin,
where meek souls will receive him still,
the dear Christ enters in.

Now I wonder, is this what Christmas is all about? Not remembering a birthday, but accepting with joy the gift of Christ unto our messy lives today, and being open to the inspiration of his Spirit.

62 Peter and John

This year, two Christmas cards have pride of place on our mantelpiece. As it happens both are from young black men, Peter, whose ancestry is Caribbean, and John, who is from Cameroon.

Peter's card says 'To Mum and Dad', because he is our adopted son. His story – and ours – is not a success story. At the age of forty, he still lives in a hostel on benefit. He has no work and no real home – an addictive personality. He has a long history of drug-taking. His life seems to be one long struggle and for us one long sorrow, except that he brightens our lives by his faithful affection.

John gives us affection too. His card says 'To Both of You'. He is a few years younger than Peter and his life is unbearably difficult and sad. John may be deported at any time to Cameroon, where he has already been imprisoned in solitary confinement and badly tortured; where he will almost certainly be killed if he has to return. In this country the government does not believe his story and he has suffered prolonged cruelty in detention. Now he must live on vouchers worth five pounds a day, he is not allowed to buy anything other than food and he is not allowed to work. He lives in constant fear which he tries to assuage through study, good humour and the kindness of friends.

Peter's and John's cards stand between our beautiful crib and the white hyacinth that is just coming to perfection. They are not placed there so that we will be reminded of them; they are rarely far from our thoughts – they are there because we want to honour them.

63 Where is Jesus?

In our church we are rightly, I think, proud of our crib. After Mass I went to look at it, along with several young children who knelt with unaccustomed reverence as they gazed at the wooden figures representing the infant Jesus, Mary and two or three shepherds. One of the shepherds looked very young. Like the children he was on his knees; an expression of wonder carved on his face.

It was a beautiful sight, moving and holy. I found myself sliding to my knees among the others, and I was happy to stay there in silence for a few moments, simply looking.

Not long afterwards, heavy snow blocked the roads and cut off villages in our neighbourhood. Television cameras took spectacular pictures around the region, and one of these I found most poignant. The cameraman followed a district nurse who had trudged through blizzards and snowdrifts to reach a housebound man. He was in his nineties and frail. The camera zoomed in to take a close-up picture. The nurse was kneeling at the foot of the man. She took his gnarled, blotched, weather-beaten hand and clasped it in her own small, delicate one.

It was a tableau that lasted for only a few seconds, but enough for me to realise that Jesus is not a statue in a crib, however beautiful, for he was there, present in that snowbound cottage.

64 Mary

I believe that Mary was a strong and passionate woman, no more meek and mild than Jesus himself was. We have only to read or hear her wonderful song known as the Magnificat to know this. When her cousin Elizabeth greeted her, Mary said, 'My soul proclaims the greatness of the Lord' and went on to describe the justice of God: 'He has pulled down princes from their thrones and exalted the lowly, the hungry he has filled with good things, the rich sent empty away.'

Thinking about Mary, I am sad that she is sometimes portrayed, in paintings, on Christmas cards and in statues as someone rather sentimental and insipid, and as the blue-eyed blonde she can hardly have been in reality.

When God was looking
for a mother for his son,
I don't think he chose
a whey-faced milksop
who drifted around
in shapeless garments
of baby-blue.

No – I think he chose a feisty girl
with a sparkle in her eye
and a ready laugh,
one who liked to sing
and loved to dance,
who sometimes wore a flower in her hair,
a fine cook
and an even better gardener,
and someone who was very, very good
at telling stories.
In short,
I think he chose the sort of mum
to make her children happy.

65 Rejoice?

It seemed like a perfect Christmas Day. Our little town was covered in a gentle layer of firm snow and the temperature was well below freezing, so that the air was crisp in the sunshine under a pale blue sky. We walked to the beach where a 'snowbow' arched down to the sea and everything was bathed in beautiful light.

The streets were almost empty, so that we could exchange greetings with everyone we met, and back at home the little birds, including a traditional robin, were eagerly attacking the fat-balls and nuts put out for them. Our gifts for each other were simple, no more than a couple of inexpensive pens and a bar of chocolate; our candle was lit next to the crib.

We had already been to Mass on Christmas Eve. We listened to an assortment of carols as we prepared our meal together. We telephoned, or were telephoned by, friends and family; everyone sounded happy.

Then we switched on the radio to hear the news. A young woman had been found dead by the roadside in Somerset, and police were investigating. We were shocked out of our contentment. At the back of our minds always are 'the people who suffer', those who, as I write, are tortured, imprisoned, desperately lonely, the victims of famine or disease or addiction, but hearing this news and thinking of this young woman's parents, brought the reality of their anguish to the forefront of our minds.

What sort of world did the child born in a stable enter? What did it feel like for him as he grew and had to face the reality of life as a human being?

What is it like now to be the only true hope for humanity?

At Christmas we listen to the old, old story. 'Look!' says Matthew, 'the virgin is with child and will give birth to a son whom they will call Emmanuel'. This name means 'God with us.' It is Matthew, too, who tells us that before his ascension, Jesus said, 'Behold, I am with you always, even to the end of time.'

Surely we can trust the promise of Jesus, that he will always be there, whatever befalls us.

66 Angels

I have, like most people of my age, grown up with the 'incarnation myth', in other words, the Christmas Story. Since childhood I have been drawn to believe in the singing angels, the humble shepherds and the three wise men with their exotic names and equally exotic gifts. I love the story from St Luke's account, especially in the King James version of the bible.

But for many years now there has been an amazing recurring echo in my mind of a line in Betjeman's well-known poem, *Christmas*, where he asks 'And is it true, and is it true?'

Logic and the desire to be truthful at all costs demands that I keep questioning and wanting to know whether all the events in this patently inconsistent and unreliable tale could really have happened. So I remain detached and uncommitted and tell myself that it is not important to know whether Luke's account is fiction or fact.

Then, unexpectedly, I hear another story. This one was told by my good friend of seventy years. He recounted how at the age of eight he was walking through a forest with his family very early in the morning. They were on the way to hear the first Mass of Christmas, and it was so early that it was still dark. The sky was brilliant with stars and the moon was full. As sudden as the song which startled the shepherds so long ago, young Peter heard the song of angels. 'I can hear it now' he said, 'I remember the words and the tune too.' Then suddenly and without embarrassment, he sang his angels' song for us, a small group of men and women roughly his own age.

Now once again I have to look at my own convictions. I believe unreservedly in Peter's experience. I think it is as real for me as it was to him. And now, instead of being eager to find the truth about the incarnation story as it is told in scripture, I feel that it scarcely matters. I believe that God became fully human, and that's enough for me, although I look forward to hearing the King James version again at Christmas.

67 Aching

My big toe is aching because I have arthritis, and it really hurts. My wrist hurts too, because I broke it in a fall. Much worse than these, my heart aches because I had a letter today from Robert on Death Row, telling me he is going to plead his innocence again, and I know his chances are minimal. At the same time my heart aches for John, because he had a nightmare again last night and he is very frightened that he will be deported, then tortured, then killed.

And yet in spite of all these pains, some trivial, some devastating, a strange thing happened to me this morning. I was walking to a friend's house, and I stopped to look at the avenue of beeches near her home. There are scores of these trees, their trunks pale silver, smooth and shining against the blue spring sky. Today they seemed to stand so bravely, naked in the sunshine. I discovered that I was aching and I tried in vain to diagnose this particular ache. It wasn't pain, it wasn't sadness, it could have simply been awe, awe which is reverence and wonder combined.

68 October

October:
hearts are thankful
not only for the harvest,
but because
the light on the trees is golden,
bronze and crimson,
sometimes the colour of flame,
but mostly, golden.
And the light on the sea is silver,
purely shining
as the little lacy wavelets
lazily lap on the shore.

69 Perfection?

It was so perfect: it felt as though we had stepped out of reality, escaped from normality and everyday stress.

The weather was perfect: blue sky and sunshine, just a scattering of cotton wool clouds and an easterly wind, fresh but unthreatening.

And the scenery was perfect: beautiful but different from the wilder country I know well. On this coast there were no frolicking becks clattering down to the sea. Instead everything was serene, almost languorous, the narrow pale blue ribbon of the little Cuckmere river sleepily winding its way over fields to the deeper blue of the Channel water. It would have been a pleasure just to stand and stare and feel the peace, but the climb along the tops of the chalk cliffs known as the Seven Sisters was too tempting a challenge.

It was not an easy walk. The green turf rolls along high above the sea, swooping steeply downhill, then very steeply up, over and over again. I was exhilarated and exhausted at the same time, and towards the end of the walk, as we were negotiating a downward track, we noticed an old woman climbing steadily upwards. As she neared us, she smiled and we stopped. She had white curly hair framing her brown face, a patterned cotton sari and a wide gap-toothed smile. As we talked, I realised that like the sea and the sky and the lazy little river at the beginning of this walk, the lady radiated serenity. I understood that her deep tranquillity was not a capricious gift of nature, a momentary glimpse of another way of being, but an abiding, joyous presence, a memory that would stay with me long after the perfect walk has faded from my memory.

70 A little child

Just about everything seems to be going wrong, in our lives and in society. A dear friend has died, another is back in detention awaiting deportation. An election is upon us, with all its lies and boasts and ambition and stress. In the churches we have discovered how paedophilia and shameful cover ups, by those most trusted, have damaged hundreds, perhaps thousands of young lives. And now in the last few days a great plume of black ash is slowly moving over much of the western world, making air travel impossible and impinging on the lives of hundreds and thousands of people.

The old Second World War motto of 'Keep calm and carry on!' seems appropriate for times like these, but yesterday we found a simpler, happier response: we went for a walk in the sunshine with a group of friends. The woods we walked through were bright with millions of wild daffodils. Our leader, who has done this particular walk perhaps a score of times, said he had never seen such numbers of flowers and never seen them more beautiful.

Feeling lightened in spirit, we came out of the woods into a lane and reached a small farm. There we met a little girl of six or seven whose name was Katie. She had a round rosy face and a wide smile which showed a gap where her milk teeth had dropped out. She stood in a field with twenty or more lambs frisking around her legs and she held one of them in her arms as people hold puppies or kittens.

The innocence and beauty of this moment seemed to crystallise everything good, seemed in spite of everything, to echo Mother Julian's words: 'All shall be well.'

71 Anselme

We approached them all on Anselme's behalf:
The Bishop of Durham,
The Archbishop of York,
The Bishop of Middlesbrough too.
We enlisted the Member of Parliament.
They all co-operated
and did their best for him.

The congregations of the churches,
the people of the neighbourhood,
were not approached or enlisted.
Spontaneously they did the best they could.
Hundreds of signatures were collected,
hundreds of letters sent,
personal appeals made to the highest in the land,
thousands upon thousands of prayers said,
but it didn't make a blind bit of difference,
Anselme was deported.

*Anselme is a real person. When he was deported, his friends felt
certain he would be killed.*

72 Gone

Anselme has gone now
gone far away to die.
He flew across the skies to Africa,
crowded, yet alone,
surrounded by the watchful eyes
of hostile men.
He went accompanied
by so much prayer,
so much love,
so much hope,
and so much near-despair.
What now, for Anselme?

73 *Spem in Alium*

Chris, my husband, and I usually pray around five o'clock in the afternoon. One day, recently, I asked him if we could postpone our prayer time for a short while because I had heard on the radio that *Spem in Alium* was going to be played in a few minute's time. Chris smiled and said, '*Spem in Alium* is a prayer.' So we sat down together and listened to it. In English the first lines read: 'I have never put my trust in another, except in you, God of Israel.'

A very unusual piece of work written by the sixteenth-century English composer Thomas Tallis, it is an unaccompanied choral piece for eight small choirs, each consisting of five voices which interweave in harmony to make a gloriously uplifting whole. I cannot imagine that anyone would listen to it without being moved.

I was also intrigued by the way those eight miniature choirs blended so perfectly, the way those forty people succeeded in working together to create such a beautiful soaring sound.

By coincidence and contrast, we went that same evening to hear a village choir sing. The choir members were all local people, mostly of farming stock, and I enjoyed studying their different faces. As a musical experience, it was about as different from *Spem in Alium* as a piece of broken glass is from a diamond.

And yet, on one important level, the same thing was happening on both occasions. Individual people were for a short space of time, forgetting themselves and everything else in their lives, to focus entirely on their part in the whole, to give of their best so as to achieve something worthwhile together.

This is what sometimes happens at a eucharist or a time for coming together for worship or the sharing of food. We can see it at Pentecostal services where everyone present is caught up for a while, not with their own concerns or the concerns of the world, but with God.

Such ways of being, though they may last for only a little while, seem like echoes of the kingdom of God flourishing in this life, now.

74 Hester

'I am so thankful that I have no-one to whom I really matter'.

Hester did not write these words out of self-pity or melodrama. It was a spontaneous statement, written seriously. I was shocked.

For this was someone I cared for deeply, loved like a daughter. I had assumed that she was not only aware of my affection, but confident in it, yet clearly this was not so.

She had written of her suffering, and towards the end of her harrowing account, she wrote this: 'Though I feel no passion or joy in my life, my ability to feel compassion has increased.' The second part of this statement is certainly true. I know no-one who gives more selfless love than Hester. But I find it hard and hurtful to realise the enormity of her loss, to think that she can no longer feel passion or joy. Maybe she will one day? Maybe, soon?

Thinking about this, I found myself asking: What in my life gives me joy? What am I passionate about? I experience joy through other people, through those I love dearly, through reading and through beauty, especially nature. My passion is for justice, and for spirituality. But I know Hester well, and I know she shares all these things. It is as though she walks in cloud, so that all her joys and passions are dimmed. Oh, how much she deserves the blessing of sunshine!

75 The builder

On the road between Leyburn and Hawes in Wensleydale, there is a hamlet called Worton. Most of the little village is hidden, but there is a house on the roadside, now rather dilapidated, which has the initials MS and the date 1729 over the door. On the side of this house a stone frame has been carved, but instead of glass it frames a stone tablet with these words:

Michael smith
Mechanick
but he that built all things
is God – Hebrews 3

I looked up this scripture reference and found that the writer of the letter to the Hebrews wrote: 'Every house has been built by someone, of course, but God built everything that exists.'

I find it touching to imagine Michael Smith, 'mechanick'. Surely he must have been proud to have built his own home and left his initials and date for posterity. Yet surely also he was humble to make, or have made, a fine place of honour not for himself but for God. How good that it has lasted nearly three hundred years.

76 Beyond Barrowburn

Now I am in my eighties and my eyes feel as though they are stretched wide in wonder. It seems odd, after a lifetime during which I have been awestruck time and time again by waterfalls and flowers and trees and cathedrals and people that astonished me, I should suddenly find myself so moved and enchanted by these particular hills.

They are beautiful, undoubtedly, but it's not so much that; it's the oddity of them and their loneliness. In this part of the Cheviots the hills are big and round and green, jostling one another like too many round buns on a tray. In the narrow valleys between the slopes there are trees fringing the burns, and here and there forests of pines and spruce have been planted on the flanks of the hills, but otherwise there is just greenness, just short-cropped turf so comfortable for the feet of walkers.

You can walk here for hours without seeing a single habitation or a single person. There are sheep and there are skylarks, in summer a scattering of wild flowers; sometimes you hear the soughing of the wind or the splash of water in a swiftly-flowing burn. But mostly, there is silence, and solitude and space.

77 Shepherd's Cross

In a wild part of Northumberland there is a cross unlike any other. It doesn't stand upright, it isn't a crucifix or a memorial or the symbol of any religion.

The cross was the inspiration of a wealthy man who wanted to help the unemployed. He gave them work, way out on the high hills, useful work. Their task was to take local stone and build four walls in the middle of a field, four walls that met in the middle to make the shape of a large cross. The cross was built to shelter sheep, for whichever way the wind blew on those heights, there was a quarter to give shelter where the animals might huddle. Like most people, when I see a cross I think of Jesus Christ, and so it was when walking some distance away that I spied the great bare cross which seemed to lie flat on the ground.

It is not, however, a 'regular' Christian symbol; it was not intended to turn our minds to thoughts of the crucifixion. This cross on the bare hillside is not a symbol at all, and yet there is a sense in which it speaks of the highest Christian endeavour: of generosity and hard work and concern for the weak. It is a symbol of the life that Christ wanted for us all, life lived to the full.

78 Resurrection

There is a wood near my home which is particularly inviting. In the first place, there is a great variety of broad-leaved trees: oak, beech, silver birch, alder, holly; and secondly, the terrain is steep and undulating so that the path sometimes takes us high on a precipitous track with a deep ravine below, and sometimes suddenly plunges downward. There is always the sound of water, because of the many becks that scurry noisily below, and after some miles we first hear and then see a high tumbling waterfall.

Years ago, when I took this walk, I was elated by its beauty and interest, until, that is, I came almost to the end and looked at the little house. It stood there, empty and forlorn, crumbling like any ruin, and lonely, far from any other habitation. I felt sad to see such desolation, and of course wondered who had lived there and why it had been abandoned.

Two days ago I walked in the wood again. The sun shone through the trees, and it seemed to me that no human being could ever be quite as beautiful as they are. I felt happy and peaceful, and then, as we neared the end, I remembered with a sort of dread, the little house. I came through the trees and saw it, sturdy and square-built, with a new roof and a garden around it where children were playing. I spoke to the young couple who had brought about the transformation and turned the old ruin into an oasis, making their living by selling coffee and homemade cakes to passers-by. I was surprised and heartened, realising the hard work and vision that had gone into this enterprise, creating a beautiful home from what was fast becoming a heap of old stones and making a place that belonged to the landscape.

79 Pain

I am lying on my bed in quite a lot of pain, feeling sorry for myself. My window is open, letting in the cool spring air, and I can see a bright blue sky with doves and gulls occasionally sweeping by.

Inside the room too, everything is bright, though not harshly so. Facing me hangs a rainbow banner from Venice with the word *PACE* (Peace) drawn in big white letters across the middle. Sunlight makes a shining patch on my bedcover. On the drawers are photographs of all my children and a small vase of irises from the garden.

Suddenly, I think of John and I remember him telling his story of pain. In the African country where he was born he was imprisoned for his beliefs. He was put in a cell and left in solitary confinement and complete darkness for six months. Every other day he was dragged out to be tortured, and many days he was given no food. The pain was excruciating.

When I think about this, of course I feel ashamed. I wonder how John had possibly borne it, and how he had came to be the thoughtful, gentle man he is, seemingly without anger, and enjoying laughter.

80 Breakthrough

'When I wake up in the morning it isn't the first thing I think about anymore.' I had not dared to hope to hear these words from my forty-one-year-old son, because the 'thing' he was referring to was heroin, and his craving for this drug, not to mention its dreadful effects, had lasted for around twenty years.

Peter wasn't conscious of making a dramatic announcement. He was simply answering my query when I telephoned to ask how he was, and seemed surprised at my euphoric reaction, and the praise and congratulations I showered on him. Clearly he has no idea how many prayers have been said, how much anxiety and stress his father and I have lived through, how much we have longed for a moment like this, how much we have dithered over what to say, how to say it, when to keep silent.

I know that the number of children whose lives are destroyed by drugs is horrific; I certainly know the helplessness their parents feel. Over the years, phrases about silver linings and lights at the end of tunnels have come to seem pathetic and useless. We came to accept our own failure and what seemed like the certainty that Peter would never change, never be able to lead a fulfilled and happy life, never have a real job or a real home.

I am stunned and grateful, grateful to God and to all those who have cared about our son, who have continued through all the long years to pray for him and remembered him as an endearing little boy.

81 Red shoes

When the Pope visited England I felt concerned about the expense, and wondered if it wouldn't have been a more powerful gesture to spend the money needed as a gift to the people of flood-swept Pakistan. I also felt considerable sympathy with many of the protestors, because some of the pronouncements of Pope Benedict have disturbed me deeply.

However, I decided to watch most of the televised ceremonies of the visit and was pleasantly surprised by the positive and sympathetic feelings these gave me. In particular I was moved by the beauty and dignity of the Service of Evening Prayer in Westminster Abbey. The magnificence of the architecture seemed to blend seamlessly with the magnificence of the robes. I felt proud that my country presents pageantry so faultlessly, and leaving aside the momentous significance of these ecumenical occasions, the colour, the liturgy and the music all contributed harmoniously to the ceremony.

At a more human level, I felt concerned for the Pope. Being of a similar age, I know how hard it can be to stand for a long time, even when all eyes are not focused on your every moment. And he seemed so frail and so tiny next to Rowan Williams, made even taller by his golden mitre.

I was emotionally caught up in this service and watched it with pleasure. But later, on reflection, I thought about Jesus Christ, whose representative on earth Pope Benedict claims to be, and I reflected on the lifestyle of the Son of God, tramping the dusty roads of Palestine. It seems unlikely that he ever wore red shoes.

82 The crypt at Lastingham

In this place words
seem frivolous,
insubstantial,
superficial.
The stones,
ancient and damp and grey,
crafted so long ago
for the glory of God,
are steeped in the prayers and tears of ages
and speak for us,
if we will only be still
and listen.

83 Tomatoes

We don't have a greenhouse, but our tomatoes are thriving. It is a pleasure just to look at them, hanging in their bunches, most of them still green. Actually it is the green ones that are the most beautiful, shining like jewels in the sunlight. But what struck me about the tomatoes this morning was a question: 'Why have these ripened before those?'

I can see seven there on the same stem, two of them are bright red and I must pick them. Two are almost red, two are just beginning to colour and one is still green. Yet all of them have been equally exposed to sunshine and warmth.

It seems that the tomatoes are a metaphor for the randomness of life. They make me think of my five natural children. Four were born strong and healthy, one died when he was only five months old. The four, two sons and two daughters, were all brought up in the same way and in the same environment, but how different they are!

Then if we look beyond our immediate circle and look at the others who cross our path, we may wonder that some are so beautiful and some so ugly, some so intelligent and some so slow, some blessed with good fortune, others suffering one catastrophe after another. No one can understand why life is so unfair and so random. We have to accept that we will never be like those we envy, and do the best we can with what life offers. If we can develop an intimacy with God and an openness to him, then he can make us, each in our own way, both beautiful and fruitful, like the very best tomato!

84 Amanda's tree

At the end of a long walk we came to a pleasant picnic site with two or three tables and benches, well separated for people to sit and eat or simply rest. Among the bigger trees was one sturdy sapling. A low fence had been erected around it, perhaps to keep out rabbits and deer, and there was a small stone plaque engraved with the words 'Amanda's Tree'. Underneath was a date some three years earlier.

To my dismay I found that someone had vandalised this private and sacred enclosure, throwing in an empty coca-cola can and an empty cigarette packet.

I felt a sense of outrage; I reached in and pulled out the offending objects. I prayed for Amanda and those who had planted the tree in memory of her. I did not pray for the vandals. Did they know what they were doing? Perhaps not, but I found it very hard to forgive them.

85 The power of water

For a long time, perhaps all my life, I have had an almost uncon-scious prejudice against reservoirs. (As I write this, I wonder if most prejudices aren't unconscious, and that's half the trouble!) My thinking, or feeling, was that natural lakes like Derwentwater and Grasmere in Cumbria and Semerwater in North Yorkshire were a beautiful part of creation like trees and mountains and flowers, whereas man-made reservoirs were artificial constructs unworthy of comparison.

However, today my eyes were opened and I saw things differently. A friend took me walking in the high moors of North Derbyshire. It was a day of brilliant sunshine as we climbed up the Longendale Valley and looked down on those five miracles of nineteenth-century engineering: the reservoirs named Bottoms, Valehouse, Rhodeswood, Torside and Woodhead. Each lake was different in shape and a different length and all were, on that day a blue deeper and brighter than sapphires, each a source of water (and so life) for the many thousands of citizens of Manchester, a city distant and happily out of sight from this remote and lovely place.

The reservoirs were the inspiration and achievement over thirty years in the mid-nineteenth century of John Frederick Bateman. He saw the desperate need of the population and the plentiful supply of water from the moors he understandably called mount - ains. Like Telford and Brunel he was a visionary; like them he knew the practicalities: how to change his dream into reality.

For me, Longendale was a revelation. I understood that as God created the beauty of nature, equally he gave to his most complex creatures, both brains and imagination. Bateman responded to this gift in full measure; the lakes he made are no less beautiful than Grasmere and Semerwater; they also continue to be a source of power and life itself to millions.

86 Humility

More than once I have heard a politician say: 'But if we don't do such-and-such a thing (replace Trident submarines, sell more arms) we could risk losing our place at the top table!' My reaction to this is two-fold: first, what gives us the right to such a position, and secondly, surely we have long since lost any claim to such a seat.

A hundred years ago, Britannia did indeed rule the waves. The British Empire was spread over a sizeable share of the globe. But those days are long gone and it's time to accept that it's some other country's turn to be the superpower, if it really is necessary to have one.

I think it was about a thousand years ago that Scandinavia held sway over the world as it was then known to the people of the west. The Vikings plundered and pillaged and murdered and raped their way to the top, greedy for land and power.

So, what now? Those countries, Sweden, Denmark and Norway, seem content to live in comparative obscurity. They have little interest in power, and they are concerned not just for the welfare of their own people, but of the whole world. It was in Norway that the Oslo Peace Accord was forged, a supreme effort to broker peace in the Middle East (no blame attaches to Norway that it was not successful) and then Norway came to an arrangement with the people of Guyana, to give them substantial sums of money in return for their efforts to keep the rainforests free from exploitation.

It is not difficult to guess what the response of the Norwegians would be should they be offered a seat at the world's top table. But isn't it time that we in Britain had the grace to learn a little humility?

87 Skin deep

Quite unexpectedly, my friend, whom I will call Harriet, died. Harriet was one of the people who have quickened and deepened my spiritual life, and given me a glimpse of what God is like. She was lovely to look at, and it really did seem as though the beauty of her soul shone through into the beauty of her face. Harriet was unfailingly serene, yet there was always the light of humour in her eyes.

Another friend, whom I will call Martin, also died. He, too, was my companion, one who broke bread with me and warmed my spirit and helped my understanding of God to grow. Martin looked like a frog.

I have been thinking about these two dear people, thankful for what I owe them both. I think I loved them equally. Of course I know that appearances mean nothing and that beauty is supposed to be only skin deep. And yet, I wonder, wasn't Harriet's face a gift extra to her wisdom, inspiring me in the way the first primrose does, lifting my heart through my senses?

88 Nellie

The other day I went to see Janet, a friend of mine who lives in a residential home. She hardly ever has visitors and when I arrive I sense that she would like me to give her my full attention. Usually, we manage to find a secluded corner where we can be by ourselves, but on this occasion there was no such place available so we had to spend our time together in a room with several other women present.

Janet talked; she is a good talker and she made me laugh, telling me oft-repeated stories of her childhood. I tried to listen attentively, but my eyes strayed across to the far end of the room where someone was crying. I watched, dismayed. The tears continued to flow down the woman's cheeks and onto her lap. I looked at her face. She seemed desperately unhappy, and went on crying uncontrollably.

I didn't know what to do. The other women in the room were watching her, but none of them made a move towards her. Most of them were in any case unable to walk. I thought of looking for a member of staff, but I didn't want to annoy Janet. Then, to my great relief, a young carer did arrive. 'Now, Nellie,' she said, 'you're soaking your dress! I'll get you some tissues.' She went out and came back with a handful of paper handkerchiefs which she handed to Nellie. She didn't speak to her or touch her, but left the room again. Nellie continued to cry.

I felt distinctly uncomfortable.

'Is there something I can do?' I asked Janet.

'No,' she answered, 'She's missing her husband.'

Soon after this it was teatime in the home and my time to leave. I walked out of the room with Janet who managed her crutches competently. As we passed Nellie I bent down and put my arm round her and muttered some consoling platitude. She looked up at me and the sorrow in her face shocked me.

We walked on. I kissed Janet goodbye and left the building. As I crossed the path to the road I felt critical of the staff in the home, but above all guilty and ashamed of myself. I couldn't get Nellie's face out of my mind. I knew the staff were overworked and disgracefully underpaid. I guessed they simply didn't have the time to stop and show some care for a weeping widow. But surely they could have done something? I could have left Janet for a while to show some kindness and concern for Nellie. But I didn't.

89 Childless

I am empty,
I am barren.
I am hurting in my longing,
in my yearning for fulfilment.
If only
I could bear a child,
if only
I could be a mother.
I am empty,
I am barren.
I am a failure,
an outsider.
As the parched earth longs for rain,
so I long for a child,
a child to nurture,
a child to love.
If only ...

90 The 'Other'

I live in a country town in the north of England where there is scarcely a black face to be seen. Most of us whites fall over backwards to be 'nice' towards anyone with a dark skin, because we are ashamed when we hear distressing tales of racist attitudes and behaviour in towns and cities of our region.

The other day I was startled when my daughter told me that Martha, my granddaughter, had come home from school in tears because she had been bullied. Martha lives in East London and attends a multi-cultural school where there are only a handful of white children. She was the victim of racism, bullied because of the colour of her skin.

Much as I dote on Martha, I could see the funny side of this. As it happens, every one of her close friends belongs to a different race. But I also felt sad, not only for my granddaughter, but because yet again I realise how powerfully fear of 'the other' leads to the aggression which is prevalent in our society.

91 The old gate

Today we have a new focus in our house. It is a framed photograph placed over the fireplace. I am very glad to see it there and for more than one reason.

The old wooden gate in the foreground of the picture leads to a field from a lane in the small village where some of my ancestors lived three hundred years ago. They were stonemasons and it is possible that they shaped and set in place the two stone gateposts; it is even more likely that as children they climbed over the gate into the field. It is rough pasture with sheep grazing, and if you stand here you can hear the beck splashing along its course nearby. Beyond the fields are wooded hills and above the hills the summer sky.

I like the picture partly because of these perhaps fanciful associations, but even more because it somehow expresses the way I want to live and hope to live, in peacefulness, contentment and simplicity. For I am an old woman who doesn't want to dress in purple, or spit or swear or grow old disgracefully: I choose instead the way of peace.

92 Peace of mind

Since the beginning of humanity there has been a need of healing, and people have striven to find ways of restoring the sick to health and the troubled to peace of mind. Today there are numerous methods of healing across the world: there are still witch-doctors and faith healers and qualified physicians. There is acupuncture, massage, homeopathy, and reiki and reflexology, counselling, therapy, relaxation and meditation. Some of these work for some people in some conditions.

But we live in a deeply troubled world; rightly we fret and grieve over the disparity between nations, over the threat of climate change and nuclear war. We feel frustrated and angry and above all powerless, and we are saddened by the hunger and cruelty, the greed and lust for power, the fear and pain of suffering that are such a part of life.

And yet however much we are aware of the dark clouds of sorrow and injustice and helplessness that prevail, yet we are still capable of real personal joy: when a child is born, when we experience the wonder and beauty of nature, when a long-held dream of a friend comes true, when we are conscious of being loved and loving.

How can we hold our lives, our thoughts, our attitudes in some sort of balance? How can we find true healing for our deepest needs? Perhaps no-one knows the answers to these questions for which so many of us seek an answer.

For myself, I have come to believe that we need to cultivate an inner serenity, such as those who have a quality of holiness have found and choose to live by. By holy people I do not necessarily mean religious people: I mean the ones, who may be Buddhists, or Christian monks or humanists or what we think of as ordinary folk, who have attained peace of mind. They have looked long and deeply into their hearts, where some find their God, and have learned to look outward upon the world and the people who surround them with true compassion.

I know it will take me a long time to achieve this peace of mind.

93 Making good

I have written about our adopted son, Peter, before and in the tenth reflection in this book I have described him as he was on a day that was particularly happy, for him and for us, his parents.

Peter has had a roller-coaster life, and often a quite precarious existence, living in various hostels and unsatisfactory lodgings. He was a damaged little boy when we adopted him at three years (now he is forty-two!) and sadly it takes very little to make him flare up in anger.

I suppose we primarily think of Peter as needy, needing our love and encouragement though not, of course, our advice! We feel sorry for him and long for him to 'make good'.

Then last night he telephoned and told us that he had met someone called Blaise who wanted to talk to us. Blaise said, 'I want to commend your son to you. He took pity on me when nobody else would.' Blaise explained that he was homeless and had been sleeping rough in the snow. Several people had passed him and ignored him, but Peter took him into the house where he has a room and gave him a bed. 'If I could make medals,' Blaise added, 'I would give one to him.'

94 The Meeting

This morning I was invited to go to a Meeting of Friends (Quakers) in Great Ayton, a village not far from where I live. I was feeling distressed and confused about my spiritual life, especially because of the terrible suffering in Haiti following the earthquake and what felt like the persistent voices of atheists and agnostics which seem to press upon me.

It was a grey, drizzly January day as we entered the building, but the moment I walked into the Meeting Room, even before I sat down, I sensed that the place was full of God, of the presence of love and goodness and peace.

There are two Quaker sayings which hold great significance for me: one was from George Fox himself who said, 'Walk cheerfully over the world, answering that of God in every man', and the other the words of Sarah Martha Baker who lived at the end of the nineteenth century and died early in the twentieth, aged thirty. She said, 'The universe is always singing, and man must learn to listen so that his heart may join the universal chorus.'

Of course both Fox and Sarah Baker meant 'person' rather than 'man'. Today I feel that it is perhaps enough to forget the words of the Pope, of Richard Dawkins, of all the institutions and their bureaucracy, and instead live by these two precepts, in simplicity and with compassion.

95 Bread on the waters

In the Book of Ecclesiastes, this sentence is written: 'Cast thy bread upon the waters: for thou shalt find it after many days.'

I never fully understood this saying until someone pointed out to me what happened to my friend Meg.

Not long after Christmas this year, Meg opened her door to find an African couple looking at her expectantly. They were smiling but she didn't recognise them. Then the man said, 'Don't you recognise me, Meg? I'm Andrew, the penniless student you helped over twenty years ago, and this is Dorothy my wife. You probably saved my life and I could never forget you.' Meg was delighted and invited the couple into her house and they told their story. After years working as a doctor, Andrew had saved enough to build his own hospital, where Dorothy was now the Matron.

It only took Meg a few minutes to remember Louis. He had come to Britain seeking sanctuary, but in spite of evidence of terrible torture, he had been returned to his own country, where he lived every moment in fear of being killed. Eventually friends helped Louis to escape over the border into a neighbouring country where he was living rough and still in danger. This happens to be the country where Andrew and Dorothy live. So Meg asked them to try to help Louis, to give him a safe place to live, and if possible, work.

Meg had found the bread she cast upon the waters so long ago.

96 Hyacinth

Last Christmas, someone kindly gave me a basket of flowers: an azalea, and small cyclamen. I was delighted, especially as they were both the cheerful red that I like, the colour of cherries, not a pillarbox red but a softer shade of brightness, cheering at the greyest time of year. But sadly, because of severe pre-Christmas frost, life for the flowers was a struggle. They never reached their full potential and the petals came near to shrivelling. But they held on bravely and, a little faded and crumpled, lasted nearly a month.

One day towards the end of January I was about to discard them when I saw an unlooked-for stranger in the middle of the basket – a hyacinth ready to open its petals. Now the other blooms have faded and the hyacinth, fragrant and the palest pink, stands tall and proud and beautiful. I have always liked these flowers and I have come to realise that they are internationally, perhaps universally, loved. In medieval time the Persian poet, Moslih Eddin Saadi wrote this verse:

> If of thy mortal goods thou art bereft,
> and from thy slender store two loaves are left,
> sell one and with the dole
> buy hyacinths to feed thy soul.

97 Senait, survivor

In the magazine of the Medical Foundation, now known as Freedom from Torture, which is called *The Survivor*, I read a poem written by a young woman from Ethiopia whose name is Senait. She is a member of their 'Write to Life' group, herself a survivor.

Senait wrote of how she felt when she first came into contact with them. 'All I carried was emptiness.' But gradually everything changed for her, and in the last verse of her poem she writes:

What could I call this joy
that gives me meaning?
How find a name that says
my blessedness, my trust?
I can say 'Halleluya' now.

It strikes me that any Christian, any Muslim, any member of any religion might answer Senait: 'The name you are seeking is God. It is God who gives your life meaning. It is his name that says your blessedness, your trust.'

It seems to me that everyone who is seeking a meaning for their lives, seeking joy, happiness and trust, is seeking God. He, or she, may not have the face we expect, we may simply experience him as a peaceful presence within us, as light, or hope, or love.

Some people claim that God is a Christian God, some even that he is a Baptist or a Catholic God, but surely this is to deny the greatness and the generosity of the One who encapsulates everything that is beautiful, everything that is good? However loyal we are to the brand of religion we accept as our own, surely we cannot deny that there is one God greater than any one faith.

As Jesus said: 'Where your treasure is, there will your heart be also.' Senait has found her treasure; she just needs to name him.

98 Gravestones

The Quaker Burial Ground at Great Ayton in North Yorkshire, is a pleasant place, a green space in the middle of an attractive village. It consists of tall trees, grass and tombstones; in other words it is plain and simple as one would expect a Friends' cemetery to be.

I first saw the graveyard when I was sitting in the Meeting Room which overlooks it, and what struck me most were the tombstones. They couldn't be simpler, just slabs of sandstone with rounded heads, every one with identical plain lettering carved with just the name and date. I found this strangely moving. It was as though those stones were making a statement: 'In death all people are equal.' But they were also a reminder: 'In God's eyes, all people are equal.'

I happen to like graveyards. I love to wander round them, noting the ages when people died, the grandeur of some gravestones, the forlornness of others, wondering about the lives of the people I could never have known, enjoying the tranquillity and in some odd sense, enjoying the sadness.

But there is no variety in the Friends' resting place in Great Ayton. I discovered no history there, certainly no hint of grandeur. The little gravestones were hardly beautiful, but they spoke to me of certain values: humility, simplicity and togetherness, perhaps foreshadowing paradise?

99 God

I am amazed how, in spite of everything, I hold on to God, or rather, he holds on to me. Life is so fraught with all kinds of difficulty for everyone, and my own inner life is unsteadied by doubt, coarsened by self-interest, weakened by cowardice and dismayed by the confidence of the atheist scientists.

In the effort to be true to myself I have to question and explore and lay myself open to uncertainty. Influenced not only by egotism, but by the lifestyle and attitudes of those who surround and impress me, I too easily lose my focus on the things that really matter.

Suffering and sorrow, 'acts of God' or acts of humanity, buffet my faith. Many of the deeply-held tenets of the church I nominally belong to, and indeed many of the dogmas of other religions too, I find impossible to accept. How, in all sanity, can anyone go along with such regulations? I silently wonder.

So there I am, adrift and miserable, alone, confused, until imperceptibly but all at once, he, she, my God, is here again. It is true, after all. He will not let me go.

100 The present moment

I stood, waiting,
looking again,
letting myself feel and breathe
and longing to hold forever
the silence of those hills and their embrace.
Then I walked away, sad,
knowing I would never see or feel or breathe again
this particular holiness,
knowing that nothing:
not memory, not photograph,
not music nor poetry
could ever quite recapture
that moment in that place.

101 Drummer boys

They keep on drumming,
these boys from the so-called
Democratic Republic of the Congo.
They have been drumming for hours,
their fingers flying so fast
my eyes can scarcely follow,
fingers that must be worn and sore and hurting,
but will have known worse pain.
Sometimes they laugh or shout as they drum,
but their concentration is fierce.
We clap and tap our feet
and then begin to dance,
acknowledging the power of
the fingers of the powerless,
brave drummer boys from the Congo.

Most people who are awaiting the results of their applications for asylum, find their days unbearably long and boring, especially as they are not allowed to work. But some find escape in creative outlets like poetry, painting and music. Many are extremely skilled in drumming and use their talents to entertain and to take themselves away into another, happier world.

102 The presence of the Lord

For a long time
I have equated darkness with evil,
because I know that God is light.
But yesterday I drove deep into the country,
and while it was still light,
I went to my friend's house.
Much later I came away
and only a few metres
from their lighted windows
I found myself in darkness so complete
I couldn't see my car
or the road beneath my feet.
I knew then that the dark was beautiful
and friendly and strangely comforting.
And I know that God, who is light,
is there in the darkness too.

102 Damselfly

I live in a town, but only a mile from my home there is a place of peace and sanctuary, a grassy bank under the trees on the very edge of the river. You can sit there for hours, watching and listening. It is a place of stillness, and yet of sounds and sights that break the silence and delight us: a deer with a fawn stepping delicately along the further bank, the blue flash of a kingfisher, the slow purposeful flight of the heron.

Sometimes I am surprised by something that gives me special joy, as for instance when I see a damselfly skimming over the water, her wings brilliant with rainbow colours in the sunshine. And then she is gone.

She is gone, but the imprint of her loveliness remains, at least for a while.

103 Reconciliation

I have a Danish friend called Erik; he is an old man now. During the Second World War, Erik, at sixteen, was an intrepid member of the Danish resistance, involved in perilous adventures which must have terrified his parents. One day he managed to tie himself to the underside of a train which was carrying German soldiers across Denmark.

Suddenly, from the carriage above his head, the sound of singing floated down to Erik. It was an opera that Erik knew well, for he loved to sing and even at his young age he had a powerful voice. So without thinking, he began to join in the singing. At the next station, the officer hauled him out from under the train and pulled him into his carriage. There were just the two of them, and as the train started again, the officer began to sing another familiar aria and signalled to Erik to join in. The young man was happy to oblige, but also apprehensive, wondering what would happen when the journey came to an end. But he needn't have worried. The German officer turned a blind eye, and Erik was able to slip away into the dark.

Music may be the food of love; clearly it can also be a source of reconciliation.

104 Seagulls

I don't particularly like seagulls, a statement which seems to shock some of my friends. But I know these birds well. They build their nests on roofs and chimney pots close to my house. In summer, when their offspring are young, they scream and cackle for hours on end, and out on the street they snatch chips and sandwiches from the hands of bewildered tourists.

But somehow, when they are flying, I feel quite differently about them. I love to watch them swooping and gliding across the sky. And the other day, out of the corner of my eye, I saw one turn his wings in a downward curve, and the movement made me think of God and the way he stoops down to us in tenderness.

105 Singing bowl

The singing bowl is struck and the waves of after-sound still me, and all of us, into silence. It is a silence which is profound, unbroken and unbreakable. We sit as if paralysed, yet we are relaxed. Our hands lie open on our laps, receptive to whatever comes. Our senses are closed; we neither see nor hear, and within moments we lose all idea of time passing. We are somewhere else, not driven, but drawn ever more deeply into that space which is both personal and communal. In this place, nothing may happen, or God may happen, or simplicity or a lightening of the heart. We stay, accepting, unquestioning, until the singing rings again and we are gently lifted back into what passes for reality.

106 Waiting

In a letter to my friend, Robert, who 'lives' on Death Row in Texas, I told him about another friend, John. I said it was agonising for John who has been waiting for days, weeks, months and now years, to hear from the Home Office whether or not he will be allowed to stay in the United Kingdom or will be deported back to Cameroon. If he is to be deported it is almost certain he will be killed.

In his reply to my letter, Robert wrote:

> Please do let John know that I can relate to him in a certain way because I'm waiting for an answer from my private investigator to see what they can find out to help prove my innocence soon, and I'm also waiting for an answer about what the Federal Court is going to decide. So see, I don't know whether I'm going to stay alive or be executed for something I didn't do. But do please let John know that I'm praying for him to be able to stay in the UK. Please do continue to pray for my situation.

It is terrible to think what these two young men are going through, and impossible for most of us to imagine what it is like for them.

107 The Cheviots

In the mountains
you can nearly touch God.
The silence is loud with his presence.
His might could crush you
but his arms enfold you.

In the stillness
there is power
there is prayer
there is life.

The spring from the mountainside,
the beck, the stream, the river
flow to the sea.
And as surely,
the energy of love flows
to the meeting of souls in the marketplace.

108 Tree

I don't think it's so much that I escape to nature. However, I go every week, if I can, in search of peace and beauty, because the world feels too much around and on top of me. It's not that I live in a crowded space; it is my own mind that is crowded and my heart weighed down by the concerns of the world and the sufferings of people I know.

It's like being thirsty and going somewhere for water to drink, like being exhausted and seeking a place to rest. On a different level, I hope to be warmed by sunshine and refreshed by exercise, but what I look for and blessedly often find, is something that speaks to me of loveliness, and within that loveliness, hope.

Hopkins expressed this far better than I can, when he wrote: 'There lives the dearest freshness deep down things.' On Monday I came across the dearest freshness in a solitary tree. It stood some distance away in a sloping field. It was November, and the leaves of the tree were the colour of glory: intermingled red and yellow, crimson and gold, shining in the sun. It seemed to me then that nothing in the world could be more beautiful, or more affirming.

109 Hunger

Every day I hold two people in my prayers. I have not met them, and never will. I do not know their names. One, or both of them, may no longer be alive.

I only know the little boy and the old man from photographs, both of which were taken somewhere in Africa. One shows a very small child, sitting on the ground. He is holding one thin arm towards a big fat well-fed man who is hurrying by, carrying what looks like a bag of food. The man does not notice the child. The child stares at him, incredulous.

The other photo shows an old man with a lined lean face. He looks resigned but happy. There was a lot of text by this photograph, explaining that the old man's family had died of starvation, except for one daughter, his companion on a long journey in search of food. A Canadian family had met them and offered to take the girl to Canada where she would be well looked after for the rest of her life. Father and daughter did not want to part. She loved him and wanted to stay with him whatever happened, but for him there was no alternative but to let her go. The photograph shows the expression on his face just after she had left.

110 Presence

I cannot see God, hear, smell, taste or touch him. But she (and sometimes it is he) is a presence in my life: in my waking, sleeping, dreaming, working and resting. She doesn't go away even in times when I ignore or forget her.

There are moments, though, when her presence seems more powerful, more real, even, perhaps, more human. Then I imagine reaching out my hand to touch her, or feel myself showered with blessings, like apple blossom drifting down from the tree. He is tremendous, this God. I look up at the wide sky, the infinite horizon, and I know they cannot contain him. Yet he is also a small, tiny, hidden seed in winter's earth, faithful and waiting.

111 January

I began writing down the reflections in this small book in January about three years ago. The collection has grown slowly, being made up of things, people, incidents and experiences which, in their influence on me, have felt like the touch of God. Some incidents came unbidden and unforeseen, sporadically and at random, which might explain some of the odd juxtaposition of some of the reflections. For myself, I feel grateful for such insights, and my hope is that they may in some way be a blessing to others.

I used not to like January much. It is such a fallow time of the year and there is so little colour in gardens, fields and hedgerows. Often, too, it is the coldest time of the year.

But in old age I have come to see January as a wonderful month, full of anticipation and promise. I want it to go slowly, because I know that the beauty of spring and early summer will appear and disappear all too fast. I know, for sure, that here in England, as long as the world as we know it survives, there will be daffodils then primroses and violets and new green leaves on the trees. There will be newborn lambs and bluebells and the birds will be singing, and sometimes the sun will shine.

Just for now, I have to wait. I have time in January to meditate on all these manifestations of new life and loveliness before they actually appear, confident that they will be beautiful, a little sad that they will grace the earth so fleetingly.

But all at once I am jolted out of this perhaps complacent patience, this determined acceptance of the way things are in January, when I see small, green shoots pushing out of the dark earth, and within days the snowdrops are here. Fragile, beautiful and pure, yes. But also the most gallant of flowers, we might almost say defiant. Regardless of cold, frost, snow, bitter winds and dark days, they come, making a statement, echoing the Song of Solomon: 'Lo, the winter is past.'

112 Speaking

I do not speak to the rose,
she speaks to me,
she whose beauty is perfection,
transient perfection,
for tomorrow her petals will crumple and fade and fall
though by some magic her perfume will linger still.

I do not speak to the skylark,
he sings to me,
and to whomsoever will listen,
he who looks so nondescript
and sings with a more piercing sweetness
than the most angelic choirboy
and soars unfalteringly
towards heaven.

I do not speak to the apple,
she seduces my tastebuds
and quenches my thirst,
she who is round and rosy
crunchy and fresh,
so speedily ravished,
her core thrown away.

I do not speak to the sun or the silver birch,
the little waterfall, the hare, the fox or the spider.

I do not speak to God much, either.
I listen. I wait.
I marvel at him and at all these things
in which his spirit lives.